Devotion and Discipline

Training for Presbyterian Leaders

by Guy D. Griffith and Ruth Faith Santana-Grace

Edited by Laura B. Lewis,
Richard R. Osmer, and
Amy S. Vaughn

Book design by Carol Johnson
Cover design by Sharon Adams

First edition
Published by Geneva Press
Louisville, Kentucky

PRINTED IN THE UNITED STATES OF AMERICA

99 00 01 02 03 04 05 06 07 08 — 10 9 8 7 6 5 4 3 2 1

Contents

About the Authors

Guy D. Griffith has served Covenant Presbyterian Church in Charlotte, North Carolina, since 1997 as Associate Minister for Christian Education. Prior to Covenant, he was on staff at First Presbyterian Church of Libertyville, Illinois, and was pastor of the new church development, Alpharetta Presbyterian Church in Alpharetta, Georgia. At Covenant he teaches a weekly class called "Bible for Boneheads." A graduate of Princeton Theological Seminary, Griffith is also a Thompson Scholar in Evangelism. He is currently in the Doctor of Ministry in Christian Spirituality program at Columbia Theological Seminary.

Ruth Faith Santana-Grace has served the First Presbyterian Church in Bethlehem, Pennsylvania, since her graduation from Princeton Theological Seminary in 1994. Today she is Pastor for Adult Discipleship and is responsible for a number of ministries including Adult Education, New Members, Small Group Ministries, Officer Training, Lay Ministry Development, Women's Ministries, and Marriage Ministry. Santana-Grace had significant experience in the public and private sectors prior to attending seminary. She served as Executive Director of the Bridge Association in Rome, Italy, worked for the National League of Cities in Washington, D.C., and served as Director of Administrative Services for the College of New Rochelle campus in New York City.

Introduction

This study guide introduces the Ten Commandments and Lord's Prayer sections of the *Study Catechism* (Questions 89 through 134) to congregations of the Presbyterian Church (U.S.A.). It is a companion piece to the *Foundations of Faith* curriculum based on the *Study Catechism*'s section on the Apostles' Creed, but also has individual and particular applications. The Apostles' Creed section of the *Study Catechism* focuses on the basic *doctrine* of the faith from a Reformed perspective. The study of the Ten Commandments and Lord's Prayer leads into a greater exploration of how the twin virtues of *discipline* and *devotion* are central to a Presbyterian understanding of the Christian life. Historically, catechetical instruction has been a primary method of spiritual formation within the Reformed tradition.

Early on in the *Book of Order* we are reminded that "there is an inseparable connection between faith and practice, truth and duty,"[1] (G-1.0304). While the Creed teaches right belief, the commandments teach right living and the model prayer teaches right loving. How we practice our Christian faith in the world matters. The twin emphasis on *ethical living and growing in the spiritual life* that is true for every believer is especially important for those answering the call to leadership in the church. Thus this study is designed with special focus on spiritual development for those growing in leadership within the local church or who are exercising responsibility in the community.

This study guide includes eight group sessions designed primarily for a one-and-a-half-hour session format, but they could be adapted for classes of shorter duration. Each session offers whole-group lecture format, small-group interaction around questions and case studies, and individual meditation and journaling exercises. The group sessions are supplemented background material and journaling space and suggestions for individual preparation.

We have designed this study guide to help those who use it to "make space for God" in their hurried lives and harried serving. It is offered to the church with the hope that those who allow their lives to be formed and re-formed by the *discipline* of the Commandments and the *devotion* of the Lord's Prayer will mature in faith, witness to their hope, and serve with love.

Contexts for Use

OFFICER TRAINING

This study guide is well suited for use in officer training for elders or deacons. The content and process will help those elected to leadership positions in the congregation grow in faith. The case studies provide opportunities for elders or deacons to reflect theologically on situations that could arise in their own congregations.

LEADERSHIP DEVELOPMENT

This study guide is a wonderful tool for developing and training leaders in the congregation. Consider offering this study for church school teachers, youth group leaders, committee moderators, Presbyterian Women circle chairs, small group leaders, or adults preparing for an extended service project in the community.

ADULT EDUCATION

This study guide is appropriate for use in an adult Sunday school class or midweek class. While especially appropriate for those engaged in any form of leadership in the congregation, this resource is suitable for any group of adults. Consider offering this course as a follow-up to *Foundations of Faith: Education for New Church Members,* which explores the Apostles' Creed section of the *Study Catechism.*

How to Use This Resource: A Guide for Participants

Devotion and Discipline: Training for Presbyterian Leaders is designed to help you deepen your faith through theological reflection. It provides opportunities for individual prayer, reflection, and journaling, in addition to engaging small-group discussions and helpful background information. Each session is divided into two sections: "Individual Preparation" and the "Group Session." Here is what you can expect in each section.

Individual Preparation

You are invited each week to prepare for the group session through reading, reflection, prayer, and writing in a journal. This work that you do at home in the midst of daily life will make the group sessions more interesting and substantive. In addition, we hope that through these times for reflection and prayer you will begin to build or strengthen habits of spiritual discipline.

Each Individual Preparation section includes:

HISTORICAL AND THEOLOGICAL BACKGROUND

After reading through the relevant catechism questions for the session, read through the background information given. This section explores the catechism questions and answers in greater depth, providing a history of Christian thought on the topics and explaining the theology. You will find that this information will both fuel your own reflection and provide a richness to the small-group discussions in the group session.

Each session includes suggestions for keeping a journal and blank lines on which to write. There are three options for your journal each week. The first is a suggestion based on the content of the session. The second suggestion involves reading through the catechism questions a second time and choosing a sentence or phrase to reflect on throughout the week. The third option is to use the optional questions for personal reflection at the end of each session to review and reflect on the material from the previous group session. Ideally you will be able to set some time aside for your journal each day and will be able to use all three suggestions each week. If, however, time does not allow or you are particularly engaged by one of the journal activities, feel free to choose only one.

If keeping a journal and a time for personal prayer and reflection is a new practice for you, you may find the following suggestions helpful.

1. Try to find a general time that you can keep each day as fifteen to thirty minutes set aside for prayer and reflection on the catechism questions. This will help to make it a habit and not just something you squeeze in when you have extra time.

2. Think about what is a good time for you. Are you a morning person or a night person? Do you have a half hour just after dinner or before your children wake up in the morning? Look for where you could best add something like this to your life, and try it out for a few weeks to see if it works.

3. Pick a place where you can be alone and free from distractions like TV, radio, and the telephone.

4. If you find that you are enjoying the writing aspect of your preparation time, you may consider purchasing an inexpensive spiral notebook, which would provide you with more writing space for your journal.

Group Session

In each group session you will find the following sections.

OPENING PRAYER

This is a time for the class to connect with one another and with God.

Key Biblical References

Class members are given scripture references to look up so that they can then make connections with the catechism questions.

Optional Biblical References

These supplementary texts are included to broaden the connections between the catechism and scripture. They provide helpful background for understanding the language of the catechism and expanding one's knowledge of scripture.

Historical and Theological Background

This section is a quick review of the material you read in Individual Preparation.

Reflections for Christians Today

This narrative section brings together the past history and theological understanding, the biblical text, and the catechism affirmations with contemporary concerns and issues. This section sets the stage for the small-group discussion to follow.

Questions for Small-Group Reflection and Discussion

This section offers several questions for discussion in small groups. One or two questions will be selected for your groups to discuss in depth rather than trying to get through every question. If the groups finish discussing these questions before the twenty minutes is up, they can choose an additional question to continue the conversation.

Case Studies

We have provided case studies to help church leaders reflect on complex and common situations with the catechism as a tool and guide. Our hope is that class members will develop habits of bringing scripture and the catechism into their thinking and discussions when making personal decisions or decisions on behalf of the church.

Closing Prayer

Optional Exercises

Each session includes optional exercises such as questions for personal reflection. These may be included as part of the group session following the case-study discussion. Alternatively, class members may use the questions for personal reflection to add to their journaling between classes. Some groups may choose to focus on the questions for personal reflection rather than on the more interactive case-study discussions.

How to Use This Resource: A Guide for Teachers

Devotion and Discipline is designed for ease of use. Everything you need to teach this course and everything students need to participate in this course except their Bibles and hymnals, or copies of hymns, is found in this one book. The group session plans are clearly spelled out for both the teacher and the students. As the leader of the group, you will be responsible for establishing the pattern for the group sessions (see track options below), keeping the pace of the discussion and activities going, opening and closing with prayer (or delegating this responsibility to a class member), asking for volunteers to read or look up scripture passages, and choosing discussion questions. The section on Preparation Prior to Group Sessions below will give you more detailed instructions for the simple tasks you will need to do to ensure that the class runs smoothly.

Options for Structuring the Course

This study guide provides a variety of options for how you might structure the course to best suit your context. Choose which of the following tracks you would like to follow before beginning the study.

THE THEOLOGICAL REFLECTION TRACK

This approach to the course emphasizes theological reflection on a range of personal and community issues. Through small-group discussion and case studies, participants will build skills and gain experience in bringing theology and scripture to bear on daily decisions. This is an interactive model, with an emphasis on small groups and practical application. The individual preparation does provide time for personal reflection as well. The Theological Reflection Track is the default approach to the lesson plans. Simply follow the sessions as they are laid out, reserving the optional Questions for Personal Reflection for students' journals.

THE CONTEMPLATIVE TRACK

If you would like the class participants to focus more on their personal spiritual growth and developing spiritual disciplines, you might consider the contemplative approach to this study. Omit the case-study discussions and replace these with the optional Questions for Personal Reflection found at the end of each session. Class members will be given ten to twenty minutes for silent personal reflection, with an opportunity to share insights with the group before closing. If you choose this model, place a high priority on the individual preparation and journaling. Make sure that class members understand that the reflection and journaling at home are integral and important parts of the course. Spend an additional ten minutes following the opening prayer for class members to share the catechism phrase they reflected on throughout the week and connections they found between that phrase and their lives. (See the instructions for Keeping a Journal on page 10.)

OTHER OPTIONS

1. If you are concerned that few of the class members will complete the individual preparation, consider reading or summarizing the Historical and Theological Background section during the group session.

2. Several lesson plans have optional activities involving music or art. Include these as you feel they are appropriate.

3. Consider rotating the leadership of the group. All the material for leading the sessions, except Bibles, is available in this book. If you prefer, you might delegate each of the eight group sessions to a different member of the class. That person would then be responsible for preparing for that session, opening the class with prayer, keeping the activities and discussions going, and choosing the questions to focus on for the small-group discussion time.

What You Will Need

Every class member will need a copy of this book, *Devotion and Discipline*. This study guide contains the lesson plans for each session as well as the relevant *Study Catechism* questions and answers, background information, and space for keeping a journal. In addition to the study guide, please make sure that every class member has a Bible available at the group sessions. We have used the New Revised Standard Version of the Bible throughout this resource. It is fine for class members to use different translations of the Bible if more convenient. You may want to have hymnals available as well. Several sessions suggest hymns to sing in closing.

Preparation Prior to Group Sessions

- Be familiar with all the components of the lesson plan. Read through all of the background material and supporting scripture passages before class, jotting down any notes or comments in the margins.
- Decide which of the questions for small-group discussion you will ask the group to focus on.
- Decide whether you will invite the group to participate in the optional exercises or not. Bring any needed supplies for art or music options.
- Mark in the margins the times you expect to start and complete each item in the lesson plan (e.g., Key Biblical References 7:45–8:00 P.M.). This will help you to keep the discussion flowing and let you know readily whether you are running ahead of schedule or behind.
- If you plan to summarize the historical and theological background, prepare notes for your presentation.

In each session you will find:

THEME

This simply states the topic for the session.

STUDY CATECHISM

Each session includes the relevant sections of the *Study Catechism.*

INDIVIDUAL PREPARATION

This section is designed for class members to complete at home. It includes Historical and Theological Background and suggestions for Keeping a Journal.

Historical and Theological Background: After reading through the assigned catechism questions for the session, read through the background information given. This section explores the catechism questions and answers in greater depth, providing a history of Christian thought on the topics and explaining the theology. You will find that this information will both fuel your own reflection and provide a richness to the small-group discussions in the group session.

Keeping a Journal: Each session includes suggestions for keeping a journal and blank space in which to write. There are three options participants might use for their journals each week. The first is a suggestion based on the content of the session. The second suggestion involves reading through the catechism questions a second time and choosing a sentence or phrase to reflect on throughout the week. The third option is to use the optional questions for personal reflection, at the end of each session, to review and reflect on the material from the preceding group session. Ideally, participants will be able to set some time aside for the journal each day and will be able to use all three suggestions each week. It is fine, however, for participants to choose only one activity on which to focus.

Here are some ways for you to help make Keeping a Journal a success for your group.

1. Read through the information on Keeping a Journal in "How to Use this Resource: A Guide for Participants."

2. Read through the instructions for Keeping a Journal in Session 1. The process of choosing a phrase from the catechism to reflect on throughout the week has its roots in Christian contemplative practices. Our hope is that through this practice participants would become accustomed to bringing scripture and affirmations of faith into conversation with their daily lives.

3. Keep a journal yourself.

4. Ask class members at each group session how the journal is going. Provide an opportunity for them to share their reflections from the journal after opening prayer.

5. Encourage class members to give this exercise a serious and thoughtful try. Acknowledge that it is often difficult to form new habits, but that the benefit can far outweigh the inconvenience.

Group Session

In each group session you will find the following sections.

OPENING PRAYER (10 MINUTES)

Use this as a time for the class to connect with one another and with

God. After prayer, invite class members to share the catechism phrase they chose to reflect on in their journal.

Key Biblical References (15 minutes)

Class members are given scripture references to look up so that they can then make connections with the catechism questions.

Optional Biblical References

These supplementary texts are included to broaden the connections between the catechism and scripture. They provide helpful background for understanding the language of the catechism and expanding one's knowledge of scripture. It is a good idea to read over these texts as you prepare to lead the class. Encourage students to read these additional references at home.

Historical and Theological Background (10 minutes)

This section of the group lesson is intended to be a review of the background material read by participants in preparation for class. You have three options for this section:

1. You may summarize the main points of the material that was read by class members in preparation for the group session.
2. You may ask for volunteers to share one or two important points they remember from the Historical and Theological Background section.
3. If your group is coming to this session without advance preparation, you may ask several group members to take turns reading the material aloud.

Reflections for Christians Today (10 minutes)

This narrative section brings together the history and theological understanding, the biblical texts, and the catechism affirmations with contemporary concerns and issues. This section sets the stage for the small-group discussion to follow. Invite several class members to read this section aloud while the others follow along in their books.

Questions for Small-Group Reflection and Discussion (20 minutes)

This section offers several questions for discussion in small groups. Select one or two questions for your groups to discuss in depth, rather than trying to get through every question. If the groups finish discussing these questions before the twenty minutes is up, they can choose an additional question to continue the conversation.

CASE STUDIES (20 MINUTES)

We have provided case studies to help church leaders reflect on complex and common situations with the catechism as a tool and guide. Our hope is that class members will develop habits of bringing scripture and the catechism into consideration when making personal decisions or decisions on behalf of the church. Divide the class into groups of three to five persons to read and discuss the case studies. You may then invite the entire group to focus on one of the case studies, or you may assign Case Study #1 to half the groups and Case Study #2 to the other half. Leave five to ten minutes for the small groups to report their conclusions back to the whole group if you wish.

CLOSING PRAYER (5 MINUTES)

Optional Exercises

Each session includes optional exercises such as questions for personal reflection. These may be included as part of the group session following the case-study discussion. Alternatively, class members may use these questions for personal reflection to add to their journaling between classes. You may choose to focus on the questions for personal reflection rather than on the more interactive case-study discussions (see the instructions for following the Contemplative Track option above). Read through the optional exercises before each group session and decide which, if any, you will include.

For Further Reading

A bibliography of helpful resources is included at the close of some sessions. You may find these useful in your preparation to lead the class or as suggestions for class members who wish to pursue a topic further.

SESSION 1

Discovering Our Life's Purpose in God's Presence

Theme:

This lesson will focus on finding our life's purpose in the presence of the triune God.

The *Study Catechism:* Questions 1–4

Question 1. What is God's purpose for your life?

God wills that I should live by the grace of the Lord Jesus Christ, for the love of God, and in the communion of the Holy Spirit.

Question 2. How do you live by the grace of the Lord Jesus Christ?

I am not my own. I have been bought with a price. The Lord Jesus Christ loved me and gave himself for me. I entrust myself completely to his care, giving thanks each day for his wonderful goodness.

Question 3. How do you live for the love of God?

I love because God first loved me. God loves me in Christ with a love that never ends. Amazed by grace, I no longer live for myself. I live for the Lord who died and rose again, triumphant over death, for my sake. Therefore, I take those around me to heart, especially those in particular need, knowing that Christ died for them no less than for me.

> *Question 4. How do you live in the communion of the Holy Spirit?*
>
> By the Holy Spirit, I am made one with the Lord Jesus Christ. I am baptized into Christ's body, the church, along with all others who confess him by faith. As a member of this community, I trust in God's Word, share in the Lord's Supper, and turn to God constantly in prayer. As I grow in grace and knowledge, I am led to do the good works that God intends for my life.

Individual Preparation

Read the catechism questions and answers above and then read the Historical and Theological Background section. Suggestions for Keeping a Journal follow this section.

HISTORICAL AND THEOLOGICAL BACKGROUND

Beginning with a Benediction

Points of departure are significant. Whether it is leaving on a journey, the first line of a new novel, or the opening scene of a television drama, how the beginning is handled often clues us into the direction, if not the destination, of our travel. Business managers and leadership consultants express this truth when they encourage corporate strategists to "begin with the end in mind."

The starting point of the *Study Catechism* is significant in that it begins with a benediction. For most people in the pews, the benediction is not the first word, but the last, coming at the close of worship as the pastor with uplifted hands pronounces God's blessing on the congregation. Why does it come here as the answer to the first question? *"What is God's purpose for your life?"/"God wills that I should live by the grace of the Lord Jesus Christ, for the love of God, and in the communion of the Holy Spirit" (SC#1).* This formulation is taken from the apostolic benediction as it appears in 2 Corinthians 13:13, and reminds us that Reformed theology holds that the purpose of the Christian life is found in the presence of the one triune God. The Westminster Shorter Catechism taught in its first question that humanity's "chief end" was to "glorify" and "enjoy" God. A Brief Statement of Faith begins with the apostolic benediction, affirming our trust in the one triune God. The *Study Catechism* begins with a foundational question and affirms that our life's purpose is discovered in service and fellowship with the living Lord, the loving God, and the life-giving Spirit.

Meeting the Trinity Anew

The core issue of theology, from a Reformed perspective, is not humanity's perils or possibilities, not even Jesus Christ solely, but God, who is the creator, redeemer, and sanctifier of all. Specifically, Christian theology's focus is the triune God, who is personally and always related to creation in three ways.[1] The *Study Catechism* emphasizes this pattern by breaking apart the three prepositional phrases of the benediction and turning them into the following three questions: How do you live *by* the grace of the Lord Jesus Christ? How do you live *for* the love of God? How do you live *in* the communion of the Holy Spirit? The questions are probing and personal. Taken together, they lead back to a reconsideration of our life's purpose, inviting us to join our voices in the chorus of praise:

> To Thee, great One in Three,
> The highest praises be,
>   Hence ever more!
> Thy sovereign majesty
> May we in glory see,
>   And to eternity
>   Love and adore.
>
>   FELICE DE GIARDINI, 1769

How Do You Live by *the Grace of the Lord Jesus Christ?*

In her excellent book on the early church, Bonnie Thurston offers a functional definition of spirituality as it applied to the communities recorded in Acts and Ephesians. Spirituality "was what the early Christians did to put into practice what they believed."[2] Their grateful response was based on the belief that they had been "bought with a price" and "were no longer their own" (1 Cor. 6:19–20). The penalty for their sin had been paid. Christ's willingness to be faithful to his calling and embrace the horror and humility of the cross showed the unmerited free love of God to a broken world. This self-giving love of the Lord sets the pattern for how Christ's followers live by grace. The apostle Paul sets out the example of the cruciform life in the letter to the church at Philippi:

> Let the same mind be in you that was in Christ Jesus,
>   who, though he was in the form of God,
>   did not regard equality with God
>   as something to be exploited,

but emptied himself,
    taking the form of a slave,
    being born in human likeness.
And being found in human form,
    he humbled himself
    and became obedient to the point of death—
    even death on a cross.

Therefore God also highly exalted him
    and gave him the name
    that is above every name,
so that at the name of Jesus
    every knee should bend,
    in heaven and on earth and under the earth,
and every tongue should confess
    that Jesus Christ is Lord,
    to the glory of God the Father.

(PHIL. 2:5–11)

John Calvin meditates on the meaning of "you are not your own" (1 Cor. 6:19). He observes: "Now the great thing is this: we are consecrated and dedicated to God in order that we may thereafter think, speak, meditate, and do nothing except to his glory. . . . We are God's: let all the parts of our life accordingly strive toward him as our only lawful goal."[3]

How Do You Live for the Love of God?

We live for the love of God by responding to the love that God shows us. God is the initiator of the covenant. As Saint John simply puts it, "We love because [God] first loved us" (1 John 4:19). The way we demonstrate our acceptance of this amazing gift is by turning away from our preoccupation with self and living for others, even as the Lord lived *"for my sake" (SC#3).*

For Calvin, piety combines reverence for God with love. Piety is our appropriate stance before God, but it is also a way of being *for* creation as the work of God and *for* the neighbor who bears the divine image. Thus, living *for* the love of God means *"tak[ing] those around me to heart, especially those in particular need, knowing that Christ died for them no less than for me"(SC#3).*

How Do You Live in the Communion of the Holy Spirit?

To borrow Calvin's language again, the Holy Spirit is the "bond" that unites us to Christ and to one another in Christ, in order that whatever is Christ's is applied to us.[4] The sacrament of Baptism is the sign of membership in the church, the body of Christ. Baptism marks us for ministry as those belonging to God. Just as the branches are connected to the vine (John 15), so we stay *in* the communion of the Holy Spirit through trusting God's Word, sharing in the Lord's Supper, and turning to God in prayer.

Presbyterian tradition has always emphasized the life of the mind in the service of God. The answer to the fourth catechism question reminds us that part of our life's purpose is continued growth *"in grace and knowledge"* in order that the Spirit might lead us to do *"the good works that God intends" (SC#4)*.

KEEPING A JOURNAL

1. Reread each of the first four questions of the catechism. Choose one sentence or phrase to "hang on to" for the week. Here are some ideas:

   • "The Lord Jesus Christ loved me and gave himself for me."

   • "Amazed by grace, I no longer live for myself."

   • "I entrust myself completely to his care, giving thanks each day for his wonderful goodness."

   • "God loves me in Christ with a love that never ends."

   • "I take those around me to heart, especially those in particular need, knowing that Christ died for them no less than for me."

   Maybe one of these, or another phrase, is particularly meaningful to you. See if you can memorize it, or at least remember the gist of it. Let this phrase stick with you through the week. Include it in your prayers, think about it while you are in the car, and remember it in the midst of a stressful situation. Look for connections between the phrase you selected and the world around you. Perhaps a conversation, a TV show, a current event, or a situation at home or at work will remind you of it. Record your thoughts and observations about this phrase and others in the journal space provided.

2. In addition to these reflections, write a prayer of praise thanking God for the grace, love, and communion God offers.

Group Session

OPENING PRAYER (15 MINUTES)

Since this is the first time you will be together as a group, class members should introduce themselves and share something important about themselves.

Have the group leader or another class member open the session with prayer.

KEY BIBLICAL REFERENCES (15 MINUTES)

Guidelines

Assign individual class members the following texts to look up in their Bibles: *Question 1:* 2 Cor. 13:13; *Question 2:* 1 Cor. 6:19b–20a; Ps. 136; *Question 3:* 1 John 4:19; *Question 4:* 1 Cor. 12:27; Gal. 2:20.

Read the first catechism question responsively, with one person asking the question and the rest of the class reading the answer aloud in unison. (See pages 13–14 for catechism questions.) Have the assigned class member read aloud the corresponding scripture passage. Follow this pattern for the next three questions as well.

a. *Study Catechism* Question 1—"What is God's purpose for your life?" (2 Cor. 13:13)

b. *Study Catechism* Question 2—"How do you live *by* the grace of the Lord Jesus Christ?" (1 Cor. 6:19b-20a; Ps. 136)

c. *Study Catechism* Question 3—"How do you live *for* the love of God?" (1 John 4:19)

d. *Study Catechism* Question 4 —"How do you live *in* the communion of the Holy Spirit?" (1 Cor. 12:27; Gal. 2:20)

OPTIONAL BIBLICAL REFERENCES

Guidelines

These scripture references are provided to expand your understanding. You may want to assign teams to find these and report back when discussing the particular question. Alternatively, you may use these for further study and reflection at home.

a. *Study Catechism* Question 3—2 Cor. 5:15; Rom. 12:15–16

b. *Study Catechism* Question 4—Gal. 3:27; 1 Cor. 12:3; 2 Pet. 3:18; Eph. 2:8–10

HISTORICAL AND THEOLOGICAL BACKGROUND (5–10 MINUTES)

You have three options for this section:

1. The teacher may summarize the main points of the material (found on pages 14–17) that was read by class members in preparation for the group session.

2. The teacher may ask for volunteers to share one or two important points they remember from the Historical and Theological Background section.

3. If your group is coming to this session without advance preparation, you may ask several group members to take turns reading aloud the Historical and Theological Background material (found on pages 14–17).

REFLECTIONS FOR CHRISTIANS TODAY (5 MINUTES)

Guidelines

Have several class members take turns reading aloud this section:

Let's be honest: we don't live in a time that is deeply philosophical. Mostly, we are concrete thinkers looking out for what's on sale at the grocery store or how to squirrel enough away to make retirement comfortable. We answer the alarm clock and head off to work or school or our daily responsibilities without spending much time thinking about the big questions of life. Questions about meaning and purpose tend to become marginalized, crowded out by the project deadline or lost in carpool duty somewhere between the school and the soccer field. Our identity is defined by who we are in relationship to others (grandparent, daughter, husband, or supervisor) or what we do occupationally (homemaker, student, teacher, manager). But our gracious God is persistent and insistent; God calls us to remember who we are and whose we are. Sometimes we call these moments of awareness "interruptions." They can be small distractions—a lengthy wait at the doctor's office or a meeting canceled at the last minute. Often they are more significant: the birth of a child, the loss of a job, the death of a spouse, a move to a new town. When these moments of reflection come, we find ourselves asking, What is God's purpose for my life?

The *Study Catechism* invites you not to wait for an interruption, but to set time aside to think about life's big questions. It invites you to hear once again God calling you into a life-giving relationship marked by discipline and devotion.

Q2. How do you live *by* the grace of the Lord Jesus Christ? We are called to acknowledge that we live under a debt and live out of a sense of gratitude. Christ's atoning work on the cross is not just for a faceless humanity, but is the supreme good news for each one personally. The Confession of 1967 reminds us of this personal application: "The reconciling work of Jesus was the supreme crisis in the life of [humankind]. His cross and resurrection become personal crisis and present hope for [individuals] when the gospel is proclaimed and believed" (9.21). This present hope enables me to *"entrust myself completely to his care"(SC#2).* Moreover, we are instructed to take up the spiritual discipline of prayer, *"giving thanks each day for his wonderful goodness"(SC#2)* in order that gratitude might grow in our hearts.

Q3. How do you live *for* the love of God? We respond to love by loving. Samuel Crossman's haunting hymn "My Song Is Love Unknown" (Hymn #76 in *The Presbyterian Hymnal*) captures the meaning behind the *Study Catechism's* answer to this question in its first and last stanzas.

> My song is love unknown
>   My Savior's love to me,
> Love to the loveless shown
>   That they might lovely be.
> O who am I
>   That for my sake
>   My Lord should take
> Frail flesh and die?

> Here might I stay and sing,
>   No story so divine:
> Never was love, dear King,
>   Never was grief like Thine.
> This is my Friend,
>   In whose sweet praise
>   I all my days
> Could gladly spend.

SAMUEL CROSSMAN (1624–84)

Love shown calls forth a response in the beloved. *"Amazed by grace, I no longer live for myself. I live for the Lord who died and rose again, triumphant over death, for my sake"(SC#3).* We are encountered again by the personal address and the personal invitation to love others: *"Therefore, I take those around me to heart, especially those in particular need, knowing that Christ died for them no less than for me" (SC#3).* The personal encounter with God's love has public consequences as we live *for* the love of God.

Q4. How do you live *in* the communion of the Holy Spirit? We fulfill God's purpose for our life as we grow into deeper communion with God through the ministry of the Holy Spirit. Just as our primary human relationships are nurtured and strengthened by time spent, communication made, and attention paid to significant others, so too our life with God needs attention. We do not make this pilgrimage alone. We travel **"as a member of this community" (SC#4),** being bound together by the

Spirit into the body of Christ. Of the many images used for the church, the image of the body most highlights the interconnectedness and mutual responsibility of those who are joined to Christ and to one another by the Spirit. A hand, a leg, a head cannot survive without the rest of the body. We journey with others who belong to God and "bear on the brow the seal of Christ who died" ("Lift High the Cross," Hymn #371 in *The Presbyterian Hymnal*). The sacrament of Baptism is the sign of God's covenant of grace and marks us for ministry.

QUESTIONS FOR SMALL-GROUP REFLECTION AND DISCUSSION (20 MINUTES)

Guidelines

Divide into groups of three to five persons to discuss one or two of the following groups of questions. We recommend that you select only one or two questions in order to have a more in-depth discussion. If your group finishes discussing the selected question(s) before the allotted time has passed, feel free to move on to another question.

1. Reflect on the opening section of the *Study Catechism*. What difference does it make that it begins with a benediction?

2. We live in a culture that values the "self-made person" who seeks to control his or her own destiny. What does it mean for such a person to learn that we have been *"bought with a price" (SC#2)*? How can the church help members *"entrust themselves completely to God's care" (SC#2)*?

3. What is so amazing about grace? What would it mean for you to *"take those around [you] to heart"(SC#3)*? How can your church help people do this?

4. What do you remember about your baptism, and how does it make you glad? The catechism teaches that you are *"baptized into Christ's body, the church"(SC#4)*. What does it mean that the church is the body of Christ (1 Cor. 12:27)? Look at Ephesians 2:8–10 and discuss how faith and good works are related.

CASE STUDY (20 MINUTES)

Guidelines

In groups of three to five persons, read the following case study and discuss the questions for fifteen minutes. Share answers with the whole group in the last five minutes.

As an elder responsible for interviewing prospective new members prior to their joining the church, you meet with Barbara. In her late forties, Barbara has just gone through the trauma of an unwanted divorce, just as her youngest child left home. Her comfortable lifestyle is considerably altered as she looks to reenter the marketplace, which has radically changed since she last took home a paycheck. She is insecure and expresses regret that she does not have more to offer the church as a member. "Everyone has been so kind," she says, "but I feel so unworthy." *As an elder, what would you do? What can you say to her that would witness to the grace of Jesus Christ? What catechism questions and answers covered in this session (Questions 1–4) seem to be most helpful in her circumstance? Why?*

CLOSING PRAYER (5 MINUTES)

Conclude in prayer, thanking God for beginning this journey of study with the class, as together you seek to find your purpose in God's presence and learn to live belonging to God. See the optional exercises below if you would like to close with a hymn.

Optional Exercises

These optional exercises may be included as part of the group session following the case-study discussion. Alternatively, class members may use the Questions for Personal Reflection to add to their journaling between classes.

QUESTIONS FOR PERSONAL REFLECTION (20 MINUTES)

Guidelines

Invite group members to reflect individually and silently on one or more of these questions. Allow at least ten minutes of quiet. Come back together as a group and invite members to share some of their thoughts. Allow ten minutes for sharing.

1. In your small group, reflect on Question 1 of the *Study Catechism,* *"What is God's purpose for your life?"* Where have you discovered your life's purpose? Is the answer provided in the catechism a help or a challenge?

2. *". . . The Lord Jesus Christ loved me and gave himself for me" (SC#2).* How can you give thanks each day for God's wonderful goodness?

3. *". . . God loves me . . . with a love that never ends" (SC#3).* When did the love of God become more than a notion to you? When did it become real? Has it?

4. *". . . As a member of this community, I trust in God's Word, share in the Lord's Supper, and turn to God constantly in prayer" (SC#4).* Which of these three spiritual disciplines—scripture reading, corporate Communion, personal prayer—is most difficult for you? Why? Which is the one that comes most easily? What is blocking you from growing in the other disciplines as well?

5. *". . . As I grow in grace and knowledge, I am led to do the good works that God intends" (SC#4).* Which do you need most growth in, grace or knowledge? Have you experienced God leading you to do good works?

COMPANION HYMNS

Choose one or more of the following hymns to sing in closing:

"O That I Had a Thousand Voices" (#475, *The Presbyterian Hymnal*)

"My Shepherd Will Supply My Need" (#172, *The Presbyterian Hymnal*)

"When I Survey the Wondrous Cross" (#100, 101, *The Presbyterian Hymnal*)

Note in each of these hymns the believer's response to God's grace provides an option for *". . . giving thanks each day for his wonderful goodness" (SC#2).*

For Further Reading

Guthrie, Shirley C. "Who Is God: The Doctrine of the Trinity." Chapter 5 in *Christian Doctrine*. Revised edition. Louisville, Ky.: Westminster/John Knox Press, 1994.

Postema, Don. "Making Space," "I Belong," and "Gratitude Takes Nothing for Granted." Chapters 1–3 in *Space for God: The Study and Practice of Prayer and Spirituality*. Grand Rapids, Mi.: CRC Publications, 1994

Ramey, Robert H., Jr., and Ben Campbell Johnson. "Spirituality as a Response to God's Providence." Chapter 2 in *Living the Christian Life: A Guide to Reformed Spirituality*. Louisville, Ky.: Westminster/John Knox Press, 1992.

Rice, Howard L. "The Experience of God in the Reformed Tradition." Chapter 1 in *Reformed Spirituality*. Louisville, Ky.: Westminster/John Knox Press, 1991.

Thompson, Marjorie J. "Hunger and Thirst for the Spirit: The Spiritual Yearning of Our Time." Chapter 1 in *Soul Feast: An Invitation to the Christian Spiritual Life*. Louisville, Ky.: Westminster/John Knox Press, 1995.

Called to Be in Right Relationship with God

Theme:

This session centers on the primacy of the Commandments for teaching us how to live rightly and the priority of our relationship with God, as reflected in the first table of the law.

The *Study Catechism:* Questions 89–103

Question 89. What are the Ten Commandments?

The Ten Commandments give a summary of God's law for our lives. They teach us how to live rightly with God and one another.

Question 90. Why did God give this law?

After rescuing the people of Israel from their slavery in Egypt, God led them to Mount Sinai, where they received the law through Moses. It was the great charter of liberty for Israel, a people chosen to live in covenant with God and to serve as a light to the nations. It remains the charter of liberty for all who would love, know, and serve the Lord today.

Question 91. Why should you obey this law?

Not to win God's love, for God already loves me. Not to earn my salvation, for Christ has earned it for me. Not to avoid being punished, for then I would obey out of fear. With gladness in my heart I should obey God's law out of gratitude, for God has blessed me by it and given it for my well-being.

Question 92. What are the uses of God's law?

God's law has three uses. First, it shows me how grievously I fail to live according to God's will, driving me to pray for God's mercy. Second, it functions to restrain even the worst of sinners through the fear of punishment. Finally, it teaches me how to live a life which bears witness to the gospel, and spurs me on to do so.

Question 93. What is the first commandment?

"You shall have no other gods before me" (Ex. 20:3; Deut. 5:7).

Question 94. What do you learn from this commandment?

No loyalty comes before my loyalty to God. I should worship and serve only God, expect all good from God alone, and love, fear, and honor God with all my heart.

Question 95. What is the second commandment?

"You shall not make for yourself an idol" (Ex. 20:4; Deut. 5:8).

Question 96. What do you learn from this commandment?

First, when I treat anything other than God as though it were God, I practice idolatry. Second, when I assume that my own interests are more important than anything else, I make them into idols, and in effect make an idol of myself.

Question 97. What is the third commandment?

"You shall not make wrongful use of the name of the Lord your God" (Ex. 20:7; Deut. 5:11).

Question 98. What do you learn from this commandment?

I should use God's name with reverence and awe. God's name is taken in vain when used to support wrong. It is insulted when used carelessly, as in a curse or a pious cliché.

Question 99. What is the fourth commandment?

"Remember the Sabbath Day, and keep it holy" (Ex. 20:8; Deut. 5:12).

Question 100. What do you learn from this commandment?

God requires a special day to be set apart so that worship can be at the center of my life. It is right to honor God with thanks and praise, and to hear and receive God's Word, so that I may have it in my heart and on my lips, and put it into practice in my life.

Question 101. Why set aside one day a week as a day of rest?

First, working people should not be taken advantage of by their employers (Deut. 5:14). My job should not be my tyrant, for my life is more than my work. Second, God requires me to put time aside for the regular study of Holy Scripture and for prayer, not only by myself but also with others, not least those in my own household.

Question 102. Why do we Christians usually gather on the first day of the week?

In worshiping together on the first day of the week, we celebrate our Lord's resurrection, so that the new life Christ brought us might begin to fill our whole lives.

Question 103. What is the best summary of the first four commandments?

These teach me how to live rightly with God. Jesus summed them up with the commandment he called the first and greatest: "You shall love the Lord your God with all your heart, and with all your soul, and with all your mind" (Matt. 22:37; Deut. 6:5).

Individual Preparation

Read the catechism questions and answers above and then read the Historical and Theological Background section. Suggestions for Keeping a Journal follow this section.

HISTORICAL AND THEOLOGICAL BACKGROUND

The centrality of the Commandments in the Reformed tradition is reflected in the fact that their exposition has historically been a component of major confessional statements. Likewise, their weekly inclusion in the liturgy of divine worship was a standard fixture in Reformed churches until the midpoint of the twentieth century.[1] The traditional place for reading the law in the liturgy, in either spoken or sung form, came after the declaration of pardon. For Calvin, this place was intended to "bring penitents to true piety, to teach them holy living by exhorting them in response to God's grace, to meditate on God's love, and to live in complete obedience to God."[2] The law is God's gracious response to the question "How shall we live?" The Ten Commandments are a summary of God's law for our lives, which teaches us how to live rightly with God and one another (SC#89).

The Reformers' understanding of the believer's proper motivation for obedience to God's law is significant. Calvin insisted that Christians should prove their faith by a life of holiness. For him, the end of the Christian life is a life conformed to the will of God, marked by ethical commitments and personal discipline. But the motivation for conforming one's life to Christ, and ethical and disciplined living, grows out of gratitude for who God is and what God has done. *"Not to win God's love, for God already loves me. Not to earn my salvation, for Christ has earned it for me. Not to avoid being punished, for then I would obey out of fear. With gladness in my heart I should obey God's law out of gratitude" (SC#91).* The Heidelberg Catechism (1563), the first Protestant creed to reach the New World, only a half century after its writing, taught that we receive the law with gratitude when it placed the Commandments in the last section under the heading "Thankfulness."

Christian theology, when speaking of the Christian life, has spoken of justification by grace through faith, on the one hand, and sanctification on the other hand. Salvation is seen as both forgiveness and regeneration, "both God's grace as mercy and God's grace as power."[3] Historically different denominations within the Protestant family have emphasized one side or the other of these two aspects of the experience of salvation. Luther and his followers have tended to place the prime focus on the experience of forgiveness, emphasizing justification by faith. Conversely, Calvin and the Reformed churches have tended to highlight the experience of God's power for renewal, and have thus emphasized sanctification.

The difference between these two perspectives can be seen in Calvin's distinctive teaching on the third use of God's law. For Luther, the primary function for the law of God was a negative function; its purpose was to hold the plumb line of God's righteousness straight and in so doing expose and condemn the unrighteous. The Commandments became a mirror held up to sinful humanity, to show where we had gone wrong and drive us to the mercy of Christ. Calvin, on the other hand, saw a positive third use of the law as a pattern for the new life in Christ for those who have been forgiven. "Because we need not only teaching but exhortation," Calvin reasoned, the servants of God will want to use "this benefit of the law: by frequent meditation upon it be aroused to obedience, be strengthened in it, and be drawn back from the slippery path of transgression."[4] The law *"teaches me how to live a life which bears witness to the gospel, and spurs me on to do so" (SC#92).* The Decalogue lays the foundation for the order of the community. The foundation is established with the first table of the law, those commandments that focus on how the covenant community lives in right relation to God.

The First Commandment

"You shall have no other gods before me." The First Commandment speaks a foundational word, a word that has primacy over all others. Like the needle of a compass that always points north, this first word sets a direction that all the other words follow.

In its positive form it is known as the Shema (from the Hebrew "hear") or the Great Commandment. "Hear O Israel: The Lord is our God, the Lord alone. You shall love the Lord your God with all your heart, and with all your soul, and with all your might." (Deut. 6:4–5). We learn from the First Commandment that *"no loyalty comes before my loyalty to God" (SC#94).* The scope of God's first word is immense, requiring a person's "whole heart and confidence be placed in God alone, and in no one else."[5] As Luther instructs:

> To have God . . . does not mean to lay hands upon him, or put him into a purse, or shut him up in a chest. We lay hold of him when our heart embraces him and clings to him. To cling to him with all our heart is nothing else than to entrust ourselves to him completely.[6]

We members of God's covenant community are thus reminded that only the living God is deserving of our worship and service.

The Second Commandment

"You shall not make for yourself an idol" is an extension of the First Commandment that seeks to prohibit images and preserve God's freedom. The central issue is "the nature of legitimate worship."[7] The issue turns on God's freedom of self-disclosure over against all human instincts to control. God's choice for self-revelation in name rather than form, in a voice we hear rather than an image we view, in a word we trust rather than a thing we touch, is a choice made to ensure God's freedom. The Second Commandment allows for no "domestication of transcendence."[8] In other words: God alone is God, "to whom alone we must cleave, whom alone we must serve, whom only we must worship, and in whom alone we put our trust" (Scots Confession).[9] Thus it follows, **"when I treat anything other than God as though it were God, I practice idolatry" (SC#96).**

The Third Commandment

"You shall not make wrongful use of the name of the Lord your God." At the heart of God's third word is the concern that God's name not be exploited, demeaned, or trivialized through our impiety and impudence. *"I should use God's name with reverence and awe. . . . It is insulted when used carelessly, as in a curse or a pious cliché" (SC#98)* reminds us that God's gracious self-disclosure in giving the divine name carries a responsibility to use it reverently.

Calvin cautions against invoking God's name for an oath unnecessarily, because it is "calling God as witness to confirm the truth of our word."[10] Similarly, the Heidelberg Catechism has understood the Third Commandment to be: "that we must not profane or abuse the name of God by cursing, by perjury, or by unnecessary oaths. Nor are we to participate in such . . . sins by keeping quiet and thus giving silent consent.[11] "Whenever the divine name is *"used to support wrong" (SC#98)* it is taken in vain.

The Fourth Commandment

"Remember the Sabbath Day, and keep it holy" continues to teach us how to live rightly with God. First of all, we are reminded that the Sabbath is a gift of God as much as it is a command. We are called to set aside a day so that *"worship can be at the center of [our] life" (SC#100)* and we can remember whose we are. The Sabbath stands as a perpetual sign of God's providential care for life. Karl Barth asserts that we are to celebrate, rejoice, and praise God in grateful response.[12] Jesus declares that the Sabbath is made for human beings, and not human beings for the Sabbath.

In the Exodus account of the command, the reason given for the Sabbath is the divine pattern of rest built into the creation story: "For in six days the Lord made heaven and earth, the sea, and all that is in them, but rested the seventh day"(Ex. 20:11). God's gift of Sabbath is a liberating word, breaking the tyranny and idolatry of unceasing work. Therefore, *"my job should not be my tyrant, for my life is more than my work" (SC#101).*

Deuteronomy's version of the Fourth Commandment calls our attention back to the exodus from Egypt and the Israelites' flight from Pharaoh's cruel bondage. "Remember that you were a slave in the land of Egypt, and the Lord your God brought you out from there with a mighty hand and an outstretched arm" (Deut. 5:15). Hence, we are called to remember that *"working people should not be taken* advantage of by their employers" (SC#101). Deuteronomy's call to remember the exodus draws us into a reflection on God's gracious deliverance and saving power. Thus the Sabbath is given not only for rest, but for making space for God through setting *"time aside for the regular study of Holy Scripture and for prayer" (SC#101).* [13]

This first table of the law focuses our attention on our vertical relation, and teaches us *"how to live rightly with God" (SC#103).*

KEEPING A JOURNAL

1. Develop a personal journal on the first table of the Ten Commandments. At the beginning of each day, recite Psalm 1. At the end of the day, affirm one way in which you have been able to keep these commandments. Confess one way in which you broke these commandments. At the end of the week, reflect and give thanks for the gift of the law. Ask God to help you with areas in which you need growth.

2. Reread the catechism questions and answers for this session. Choose one sentence or phrase to "hang on to" for the week. Here are some ideas:

   • "With gladness in my heart I should obey God's law out of gratitude, for God has blessed me by it and given it for my well-being."

   • "Why should you obey this law?" "Not to win God's love, for God already loves me."

   • "My job should not be my tyrant, for my life is more than my work."

   • "It is right to honor God with thanks and praise, and to hear and receive God's Word, so that I may have it in my heart and on my lips, and put it into practice in my life."

   Maybe one of these, or another phrase, is particularly meaningful to you. See if you can memorize it, or at least remember the gist of it. Let this phrase stick with you through the week. Include it in your prayers, think about it while you are in the car, and remember it in the midst of a stressful situation. Look for connections between the phrase you selected and the world around you. Perhaps a conversation, a TV show, a current event, or a situation at home or at work will remind you of it. Record your thoughts and observations about this phrase and others in the journal space provided.

3. Consider using the Questions for Personal Reflection at the end of Session 1 (pages 24–25) to reflect on last week's material if you did not already complete this exercise in class.

Group Session

OPENING PRAYER (5 MINUTES)

Have the group leader or another class member open the session with prayer. Invite those who are willing to share the catechism phrase they focused on in their journaling.

KEY BIBLICAL REFERENCES (15 MINUTES)

Guidelines

Assign individual class members the catechism questions and accompanying scripture passages listed below. (See pages 26–28 for catechism questions.) Read catechism Question 89 responsively, with one person asking the question and the rest of the class reading the answer aloud in unison. Have the assigned class member read aloud the corresponding scripture passages. Follow this pattern for Questions 90–103 as well.

a. *Study Catechism* Question 89—"What are the Ten Commandments?" (Matt. 19:17)

b. *Study Catechism* Question 90—"Why did God give this law?" (Ex. 20:2; Luke 1:74–75)

c. *Study Catechism* Question 91—"Why should you obey this law?" (Ps. 118:1)

d. *Study Catechism* Question 92—"What are the uses of God's law?" (Rom. 3:20, 7:7; Prov. 6:23)

e. First Commandment: *Study Catechism* Questions 93 and 94—"You shall have no other gods before me." (Ex. 20:3, Deut. 5:7)

f. Second Commandment: *Study Catechism* Questions 95 and 96—"You shall not make for yourself an idol." (Ex. 20:4; Deut. 5:8)

g. Third Commandment: *Study Catechism* Questions 97 and 98—"You shall not make wrongful use of the name of the Lord your God." (Ex. 20:7; Deut. 5:11)

h. Fourth Commandment: *Study Catechism* Questions 99–103—"Remember the Sabbath Day, and keep it holy." (Ex. 20:8; Deut. 5:12)

OPTIONAL BIBLICAL REFERENCES

Guidelines

These scripture references are provided to expand your understanding. You may want to assign teams to find these and report back when discussing the particular question. Alternatively, you may use these for further study and reflection at home.

a. First Commandment: Deut. 6:4–5; Prov. 9:10; Matt. 6:24, 10:37

b. Second Commandment: Deut. 6:14; 1 John 5:21; Ex. 34:14; Rom. 1:22

c. Third Commandment: Pss. 29:2, 103:1–2, 138:2; Rev. 15:3–4; Eph. 4:29

d. Fourth Commandment: Rom. 10:8; Gen. 2:3; Lev. 23:3; Acts 2:42,46; Deut. 5:14; Ex. 31:17; Mark 16:2; Acts 4:33, 20:7

HISTORICAL AND THEOLOGICAL BACKGROUND (5–10 MINUTES)

You have three options for this section:

1. The teacher may summarize the main points of the material (found on pages 28–32) that was read by class members in preparation for the group session.

2. The teacher may ask for volunteers to share one or two important points they remember from the Historical and Theological Background section.

3. If your group is coming to this session without advance preparation, you may ask several group members to take turns reading aloud the Historical and Theological Background material (found on pages 28–32).

REFLECTIONS FOR CHRISTIANS TODAY (10 MINUTES)

Guidelines

Have several class members take turns reading this section aloud.

We live in a time of chaos. Everywhere we look we see the effects of *dis*-ease, disorder, and distress. In the cities, many ordinary people now live as prisoners in their own homes, locked behind bars over their windows and bolts on their doors. In the suburbs, "gated communities" seek to create pockets of protection from the ills of our age, but inside the neat cul-de-sac homes family life is torn apart by divorce, neglect, and abuse. Traditional institutions of stability—government, schools, church—are replete with controversy and seem unresponsive to aching human need. The marketplace demands more of our time and energy as the pressure of international competition increases. In the midst of the chaos of our time, the Ten Commandments stand out as a beacon lighting a way of hope. They are laws that liberate and *"teach us how to live rightly with God and one another" (SC#89).*

Q90. Why did God give this law? We are reminded that God gave the law not as a burden, but to be a blessing for the community. It is a foundational *"charter of liberty"* for how children of the covenant should live with God and one another. These "commands and prohibitions were not presented to the community as harsh and onerous impositions, but as loving protections safeguarding this space for fellowship with God."[14] The catechism calls our attention to the fact that God gave the Commandments to *a people chosen to live in covenant with God and to serve as a light to the nations."* In the midst of a culture in chaos, what would it mean for the church to become a "light to the nations"? Or even within the church, for the session or board of deacons, those who have been called by the voice of the church to *"love, know, and serve the Lord today"* to discipline their lives by the law?

Q91. Why should you obey this law? We are invited to lay down the burden of our striving for approval, our self-justification, and our fear of punishment as a motivation for obeying the law. *"Not to win God's love, for God already loves me. Not to earn my salvation, for Christ has earned it for me. Not to avoid being punished, for then I would obey out of fear."* This answer places us at the very heart of the gospel. For those who claim that "the Old Testament is filled with law and the New Testament is filled with grace," this answer points to the gracious God who steadfastly loves the covenant people from Genesis through Revelation. Moreover, we discover our true motivation for discipleship: *"With gladness in my heart I should obey God's law out of gratitude, for God has blessed me by it and given it for my well-being."*

Q92. What are the uses of God's law? We encounter at this question a distinctive Presbyterian and Reformed teaching about the third use of the law. Until Calvin, Christians understood the law mostly as bad news, either showing them how far from God's will they were living or restraining their sinful impulses out of fear of punishment. Calvin opened a new way of understanding the law, which claimed that the law *"teaches me how to live a life which bears witness to the gospel, and spurs me on to do so."* This commitment to sanctification in the Christian life within the Reformed family of churches has sometimes led to a legalistic, self-righteous pharisaism. To guard against this tendency, Calvin reminds his readers not to stop at the Ten Commandments only, but to press on to our Lord's Sermon on the Mount; on the mountainside Jesus teaches that God's intent is to write the law inwardly on our hearts so that our lives would model God's grace.

In the First Commandment—"You shall have no other gods before me"—we are called to put first things first. In a world of competing loyalties, each clamoring for our time and affections, this first word stands before all others: *"No loyalty comes before my loyalty to God."* Not self-image or success. Not family or friends. Not church work or charity. God comes first. The First Commandment requires us, even in our community life, to keep our eyes focused on God alone.

In the Second Commandment—"You shall not make for yourself an idol"—we are confronted with the logical extension of God's first word prohibiting other gods. We cannot hem in the transcendent God through a thing we touch or an image we view. The second word warns us not to mistake a golden "guardian angel" pin worn on a lapel, or a perfect sunrise seen from a mountaintop, as God, even if they may be a source of turning our thoughts toward God.

Moreover, we are cautioned to keep in perspective our own narrow interests. For *"when I assume that my own interests are more important than anything else, I make them into idols, and in effect make an idol of myself."* None of us can claim that our own perspective is definitively the mind of Christ. We do well to avoid this form of idolatry when we heed the apostle's advice: "Let each of you look not to your own interests, but to the interests of others" (Phil. 2:4).

In the Third Commandment—"You shall not make wrongful use of the name of the Lord your God"—we are confronted with the issue of reverence and awe. American society is known throughout the world as a casual culture. Casual acquaintances assume an openness and accessibility in relationship that in other cultures is reserved only for a handful of intimate friends. Children address adults by their first names; political leaders and presidents are lampooned nightly. Perhaps in a democracy all social relationships ultimately get flattened out. But not so with God. Honoring God's name by giving it the awe and reverence it is due reminds us that we have no other god before Yahweh. The Third Commandment is an extension of the First.

The *Study Catechism* reminds us as well that God's name *"is taken in vain when used to support wrong."* We need to look no farther back in history than apartheid in South Africa or Jim Crow laws in our own country to see examples of the church defending unjust practices in God's name. The Crusades in the eleventh through thirteenth centuries, and the capitulation by German Christians to Nazism in our own century, provide additional examples. Jesus reminds us that it is always easier to see the speck of dust in our brother's or sister's eye than the log in our own. Looking back on history enables us to see clearly the misuse of God's name, but we must watch for this in our own time and place as well. The commandment and catechism caution us to be diligent in how we invoke the Divine name, for *"it is insulted when used carelessly."*

In the Fourth Commandment—"Remember the Sabbath Day, and keep it holy"—we come face to face with an immense challenge. Barely a generation ago, Sabbath keeping was supported by municipal laws and societal custom. The present generation knows nothing of this gentler time in its rush to the soccer field or the shopping mall. We cannot turn back the hands of time, nor would we if we could. How then do we make space for God in our lives? *"In worshiping together on the first day of the week, we celebrate our Lord's resurrection, so that the new life Christ brought us might begin to fill our whole lives."* Worshiping with the community is one way we make room for God. We do well to avoid having other church responsibilities stand in the way of the priority of worship. Another way we make room for God is by taking worship into our homes, by putting *"time aside for the regular study of Holy Scripture and for prayer, not only by myself but also with others, not least those in my own household."* We also need rest, a cessation from our labor. The blessing of such rest is aptly described by the poet John Greenleaf Whittier:

> O Sabbath rest by Galilee,
>   O calm of hills above,
> Where Jesus knelt to share
>   with Thee
> The silence of eternity,
>   Interpreted by love!
>
> Drop Thy still dews of quietness,
>   Till all our strivings cease;
> Take from our souls the strain
>   and stress,
> And let our ordered lives confess
>   The beauty of Thy peace.

JOHN GREENLEAF WHITTIER, 1872[15]

Can the church present any better witness to a culture in chaos than to "let our ordered lives confess / The beauty of [God's] peace"? The commandments teach us *"how to live rightly with God."*

QUESTIONS FOR SMALL-GROUP REFLECTION AND DISCUSSION
(20 MINUTES)

Guidelines

Divide into groups of three to five persons to discuss one or two of the following questions. We recommend that you select only one or two questions in order to have a more in-depth discussion. If your group finishes discussing the questions before the allotted time has passed, feel free to move on to another question.

1. Reflect on one of the four commandments discussed. Share how you as a community can work to obey that commandment more fully. Be specific about your ideas.

2. Reflecting on the *Study Catechism* questions and answers #89–#92 (the preface to the Commandments), share one new thought or understanding that you discovered.

3. In a culture in chaos, what can your community of faith do to help people understand that God's *"great charter of liberty"* is intended to help the church to become *"a light to the nations"*? What would it mean for your church to become a "light" to your community?

4. Why is it important for your session or board of deacons to be clear about the priority of the First Commandment? How could they live this out?

5. How does your community of faith help people keep the Sabbath? If your church follows the liturgical calendar, how does it resolve the tension between *"celebrat[ing] our Lord's resurrection"* each Sunday and observing the particular rhythms, seasons, and feast days of the church year? Is there a tension?

6. In what way is your community of faith enabling people *"to put time aside for the regular study of Holy Scripture and for prayer"* in small groups or with their families? Are there ways this ministry could be strengthened?

CASE STUDIES (20 MINUTES)

Guidelines

Divide the class into groups of three to five persons to read and discuss the following case studies. Assign Case Study #1 to half the groups and Case Study #2 to the other half.

1. The Flemings are new to town. Their prior church experience was significant, and their former pastor recommended to them your church. Their three children range in age from a ninth grader to a nine-year-old to a newborn. As you greet them in the pew they are excited to learn you are an elder because, as they say, "We have a few questions about the way you do things here." After worship the questions come: "When we took our baby to the nursery, we noticed that a lot of teenaged girls were helping out. When we asked one about Sunday school for our ninth grader, she told us that most of

the senior high girls work in the nursery and most of the guys meet with a teacher during worship. Then we saw the ushers leave with the offering, but they never came back to rejoin worship. And during the announcement time in worship, the pastor said three committees and the session are all meeting after worship for their regular meetings. Isn't Sunday supposed to be a day for worship and rest? It doesn't seem like either are a high priority here! Are they?" *How would you answer their concerns? What are some of the challenges involved in church planning, and how do you determine which takes priority? What catechism questions and answers, biblical texts, and commandments seem to speak to this situation? Why?*

2. You have been called on to help teach the confirmation class for the semester. The task of taking the twelve confirmands through the Ten Commandments is daunting enough, but what makes it worse is that it is *this particular* group of twelve. Their reputation precedes them. Among the Sunday school teachers they've earned the nickname "the Disciples." The name was given not for their piety, but because they jostle for attention just like the sons of Zebedee (Mark 10:35) and fight among themselves. Nevertheless, they are relatively civil to you when class begins. But when you start to talk about God's law, one of the girls bursts out, "Rules, rules, rules! That's all there ever is. God is so mean! Like, why can't God just lighten up?" *Where in the* **Study Catechism** *can you go to begin to formulate an answer? How does Calvin's third use of the law provide a different way of looking at "rules, rules, rules"?*

CLOSING PRAYER (5 MINUTES)

Stand in a circle and join hands. The teacher or another class member may lead the group in a bidding prayer of thanksgiving. Ask each person to respond with a one-word petition after the prompt, "Lord, we praise your name for . . ." An example is: "Lord, we praise your name for . . ." "Your grace." "Lord, we praise your name for . . ." "This group." Close with the Lord's Prayer.

Optional Exercises

These optional exercises may be included as part of the group session following the case-study discussion. Alternatively, class members may use the questions for personal reflection to add to their journaling between classes.

Guidelines

Invite group members to reflect individually and silently on one or more of these questions. Allow at least ten minutes of quiet. Come back together as a group and invite members to share some of their thoughts. Allow ten minutes for sharing.

1. How have you understood the Ten Commandments in the past—as a burden or a blessing? Are you at the point where you understand the motivation for obedience to them as gratitude? Reread Question and answer #91.

2. What other gods compete for your loyalty? What can you do to keep God's primacy a priority? Are there ways your community of faith or your family can help you?

3. Have you ever made an idol of yourself by assuming your interests were more important than anything else? Write a prayer of confession to God asking for forgiveness.

4. In a casual culture, how can you learn to use God's name with reverence and awe? Can you discipline yourself not to use it *"carelessly, as in a curse or pious cliché"*?

5. What would it take for Sabbath keeping to happen in your life or in your family? How is your job tyrannical, and what would need to change for it to become less so?

6. What does it mean for you that we worship on the first day of the week to *"celebrate our Lord's resurrection"*? How does that change your understanding of worship?

For Further Reading

Bass, Dorothy, ed. "Keeping Sabbath." Chapter 6 in *Practicing Our Faith.* San Francisco: Jossey-Bass, 1997.

Killinger, John. "The Key to a Good Life: The Real Story of the Ten Commandments." Chapter 1 in *To My People with Love*. Nashville: Abingdon Press, 1988.

Leith, John H. "Faith and Doctrine," "Christian Freedom," and "The Law and Moral Decisions." Chapters 2, 15, and 16 in *Basic Christian Doctrine.* Louisville, Ky.: Westminster/John Knox Press, 1993.

Rice, Howard L. "The Discipline of the Christian Life." Chapter 7 in *Reformed Spirituality.* Louisville, Ky.: Westminster/John Knox Press, 1991.

Called to Be in Right Relationship with One Another

Theme:

This session will focus on understanding that we are called to respect and cherish our relationships with others, as reflected in the Fifth, Sixth, and Seventh Commandments.

The *Study Catechism:* Questions 104–110

Question 104. What is the fifth commandment?

"Honor your father and your mother" (Ex. 20:12; Deut. 5:16).

Question 105. What do you learn from this commandment?

Though I owe reverence to God alone, I owe genuine respect to my parents, both my mother and father. God wills me to listen to them, be thankful for the benefits I receive from them, and be considerate of their needs, especially in old age.

Question 106. Are there limits to your obligation to obey them?

Yes. No mere human being is God. Blind obedience is not required, for everything should be tested by loyalty and obedience to God. When it seems as though I should not obey, I should always be alert to possible self-deception on my part and should pray that we may all walk in the truth of God's will.

Question 107. What is the sixth commandment?

"You shall not murder" (Ex. 20:13; Deut. 5:17).

Question 108. What do you learn from this commandment?

God forbids anything that harms my neighbor unfairly. Murder or injury can be done not only by direct violence but also by an angry word or a clever plan, and not only by an individual but also by unjust social institutions. I should honor every human being, including my enemy, as a person made in God's image.

Question 109. What is the seventh commandment?

"You shall not commit adultery" (Ex. 20:14; Deut. 5:18).

Question 110. What do you learn from this commandment?

God requires fidelity and purity in sexual relations. Since love is God's great gift, God expects me not to corrupt it or confuse it with momentary desire or the selfish fulfillment of my own pleasures. God forbids all sexual immorality, whether in married or in single life.

Individual Preparation

Read the catechism questions and answers above and then read the Historical and Theological Background section. Suggestions for Keeping a Journal follow this section.

HISTORICAL AND THEOLOGICAL BACKGROUND

The first four commandments focus on the relationship of a covenant God with the children of Israel, primarily exploring the question: How are the faithful to relate to their God? The focus of the commandments now shifts to the covenant community of believers and their relationship to one another and to others. The question becomes: How are the faithful children of God to behave with regard to one another? What is the appropriate attitude for the children of God in their daily interaction with others?

The Fifth Commandment

The Fifth Commandment, "Honor your father and your mother," addresses the most basic covenantal human relationship—that of parent and child. We have all either been or continue to be a child of parents. No one escapes this reality. Parents are agents who, by the grace of God, bring forth new life into the world. According to Martin Luther, God "distinguishes father and mother above all other persons on earth, and places them next to himself."[1] It is no wonder that we are called to "honor" our parents. ***God wills me to listen to them, be thankful for the benefits I receive from them, and be considerate of*** *their needs, especially in old age" (SC #105).* John Calvin reminds us that we are "forbidden to detract from their dignity either by contempt, by stubbornness, or by ungratefulness."[2]

It should be noted that father and mother are given the same importance in this commandment. This should not be lost as an insignificant detail. The commandments were written at a historical time when women were considered property. The message here is intentional. The role of mother is valued as having a key role in the shaping and nurturing of the young lives that would grow to be responsible and contributing adult members of the covenant community.

The Sixth Commandment

We now move from the commandment that seeks to value and protect the most basic human relationship to the commandment that seeks to preserve and respect all human life—"You shall not murder." Jesus was clear in his teaching and understanding of this commandment: "You have heard that it was said to those of ancient times, 'You shall not murder'; and 'whoever murders shall be liable to judgment.' But I say to you that if you are angry with a brother or sister, you will be liable to judgment; and if you insult a brother or sister, you will be liable to the council: and if you say, 'You fool,' you will be liable to the hell of fire" (Matt. 5:21–22). Jesus widens the understanding of this commandment to include inner emotional life and gossip that could lead to murdering or killing another person's spirit. *"God forbids anything that harms my neighbor unfairly. Murder or injury can be done not only by direct violence but also by an angry word or a clever plan, and not only by an individual but also by unjust social institutions" (SC#108).*

The negative imperative of this commandment invites us to reflect on the positive implications for the life of the faithful. If one is not to "murder" another—physically, emotionally, or psychologically—what then is our responsibility for the preservation of life in this world? It is not enough to sit back passively with regard to this commandment. Luther admonishes, "This commandment is violated not only when a person actually does evil, but also when he fails to do good."[3] Members of the covenant community are called to be active agents of life. We are to clothe ourselves with "compassion, kindness, humility, meekness, and patience" (Col. 3:12). We are to live our lives concerned with the well-being of everyone around us. It is not sufficient to care only for ourselves and for those we love. *We are called to "honor every human being, including my enemy, as a person made in God's image" (SC#108).*

The Seventh Commandment

The Seventh Commandment focuses on the relationship between men and women in the covenant of marriage—"You shall not commit adultery." Adultery was understood as the sexual activity of either one of the partners (wife or husband) with another outside that covenantal relationship. Breaking this commandment was a crime punishable by death (Deut. 22:22). Adultery violates God's intent for the relationship between man and woman, a relationship based on love and trust within the covenant of marriage. According to Luther, God established marriage "as the first of all institutions, and . . . created man and woman differently (as is evident), not for lewdness, but to be true to each other, be fruitful, beget children, and support and bring them up to the glory of God."[4] Faithfulness and loyalty are critical to the health of covenant life. *"God requires fidelity and purity in sexual relations"(SC#110).* Without faithfulness and loyalty, it is impossible for a relationship to grow in the kind of love and trust that can lead to true intimacy.

In the Gospel of Matthew, Jesus challenged and expanded the Old Testament understanding of adultery to include adultery of the heart—"I say to you that everyone who looks at a woman with lust has already committed adultery with her in his heart" (Matt. 5:27–28). We are called to fidelity and purity in all our relations with others. *"Since love is God's great gift, God expects me not to corrupt it, or confuse it with momentary desire or the selfish fulfillment of my own pleasures. God forbids all sexual immorality, whether in married or in single life" (SC#110).*

KEEPING A JOURNAL

1. Continue your personal journal on the Ten Commandments, focusing this week on commandments five, six, and seven. At the beginning of each day, recite Psalm 1. At the end of the day, affirm one way in which you have been able to keep these commandments. Confess one way in which you broke these commandments. At the end of the week, reflect and give thanks for the gift of the law. Ask God to help you with areas in which you need growth.

2. Reread the catechism questions and answers for this session. Choose one sentence or phrase to "hang on to" for the week. Here are some ideas:

   • "I should honor every human being, including my enemy, as a person made in God's image."

- "Since love is God's great gift, God expects me not to corrupt it, or confuse it with momentary desire or the selfish fulfillment of my own pleasures."
- "No mere human being is God."
- "I owe genuine respect to my parents, both my mother and father."

Maybe one of these, or another phrase, is particularly meaningful to you. See if you can memorize it, or at least remember the gist of it. Let this phrase stick with you through the week. Include it in your prayers, think about it while you are in the car, and remember it in the midst of a stressful situation. Look for connections between the phrase you selected and the world around you. Perhaps a conversation, a TV show, a current event, or a situation at home or at work will remind you of it. Record your thoughts and observations about this phrase and others in the journal space provided.

3. Consider using the Questions for Personal Reflection at the end of Session 2 (page 42) to reflect on last week's material if you did not already complete this exercise in class.

Group Session

OPENING PRAYER (5 MINUTES)

Have the group leader or another class member open the session with prayer. Invite those who are willing to share the catechism phrase they focused on in their journaling.

KEY BIBLICAL REFERENCES (15 MINUTES)

Guidelines

Assign individual class members the catechism questions and accompanying scripture passages listed below. Read catechism Questions 104–106 responsively, with one person asking the question and the rest of the class reading the answer aloud in unison. (See page 43 for catechism questions.) Have the assigned class member read aloud the corresponding scripture passages. Follow this pattern for Questions 107–110 as well.

a. Fifth Commandment: *Study Catechism* Questions 104–106 (Ex. 20:12; Deut. 5:16)

b. Sixth Commandment: *Study Catechism* Questions 107–108 (Ex. 20:13; Deut. 5:17)

c. Seventh Commandment: *Study Catechism* Questions 109–110 (Ex. 20:14; Deut. 5:18)

OPTIONAL BIBLICAL REFERENCES

Guidelines

These scripture references are provided to expand your understanding. You may want to assign teams to find these and report back when discussing the particular question. Alternatively, you may use these for further study and reflection at home.

a. Fifth Commandment: Eph. 5:21; 6:2; Rom. 12:10; 1 Peter 2:17

b. Sixth Commandment: Matt. 5:21–22; 1 John 3:15; Col. 3:12–13

c. Seventh Commandment: Matt. 5:27–29; Heb. 13:4; 1 Thess. 4:3–4

HISTORICAL AND THEOLOGICAL BACKGROUND (5 -10 MINUTES)

You have three options for this section:

1. The teacher may summarize the main points of the material (found on pages 44–46) that was read by class members in preparation for the group session.

2. The teacher may ask for volunteers to share one or two important points they remembered from the Historical and Theological Background section.

3. If your group is coming to this session without advance preparation, you may ask several group members to take turns reading aloud the Historical and Theological Background material (found on pages 44–46).

REFLECTIONS FOR CHRISTIANS TODAY (5 MINUTES)

Guidelines

Have several class members take turns reading this section aloud.

In a culture that does not necessarily value covenants, it is more important than ever for Christians to reclaim our biblical heritage of covenant life. High divorce rates and fragmented family systems are but symptoms of the lack of commitment that is prevalent in our society. We must either visibly take the lead in turning this noncovenantal tide and trend, or passively sit back and watch it continue to destroy the fabric of our culture. It is by divine intent that we are each related and connected to the other. We cannot escape that reality. One person's breach of any of these commandments causes a domino effect on the lives of countless others. John Calvin noted that "the Lord has bound mankind together by a certain unity, hence each man ought to concern himself with the safety of all."[5] "Honor your father and your mother," "You shall not murder," and "You shall not commit adultery" call us to preserve and cherish the dignity of life by being in right relationship with one another and our neighbor in the world.

In the Fifth Commandment—"Honor your father and your mother"—we are called to preserve the relationship between parent and child that is so basic to the development of all individuals. No gift is greater than the gift of love many of us receive from our mothers and/or fathers. It is in gratefulness for their loving faithfulness to us that we, in joy, respond with thanksgiving, care, respect, and love. This is especially important as parents become elderly and health begins to fail them.

Just as there is no greater foundation to a healthy emotional life than loving parents, there is also no greater emotional devastation than the one resulting from the absence or misuse of parental love. There is no escaping the reality that many of us have grown up in "less than perfect" homes with "'less than perfect" parents. Moreover, there are some who have grown up with parents who have actively participated in abuse. It is under these difficult circumstances that we must too often find the courage to resist the blind obedience that this commandment might at first glance imply. *"Blind obedience is not required, for everything should be tested by loyalty and obedience to God. When it seems as though I should not obey, I should always be alert to possible self-deception on my part and should pray that we may all walk in the truth of God's will" (SC#106).* At those painful times that human behavior destroys the dignity of a person, we are reminded that "we must obey God rather than any human authority" (Acts 5:29).

In the Sixth Commandment—"You shall not murder"—we are called to preserve the gift of human life. This commandment is a reminder that we are made "good" in the image of God (Gen. 1:27, 31). As such, we are not to allow anything or anyone to diminish the value of that life. This is especially true when we are angry and in conflict with others. At those times, it is easy for us to disregard the other. It is easy for us to think or speak badly of "the other." And yet we are commanded to find compassion for others—even those who have wronged us. "Do not rejoice when your enemies fall, and do not let your heart be glad when they stumble" (Prov. 24:17).

This commandment invites us to cherish human life as a gift and blessing from God. We are to treat all God's children throughout the world with respect and fairness. We are to be active agents of change wherever and whenever others are being mistreated. "It is not enough for a community's life and health simply to avoid crimes."[6] We are not free to sit back and watch injustice, believing that in this manner we can remain guilt-free. We must embody this respect for human life and seek to promote it in the workplace, in the playground, at home, at school, throughout our nation and in the international community as well.

In the Seventh Commandment—"You shall not commit adultery"—we are called to preserve the relationship between man and woman within the covenantal bond of marriage. Today, more than ever, it is possible for us to be adulterous in our relationships without sexual activity. Adultery can be considered anything that physically and/or emotionally takes you away from your primary relationship with your spouse. Success, power, money, sports, television, and the computer are just a few examples of the popular cultural distractions that keep us disconnected from our primary relationship. We are to work diligently toward creating and building trust within our primary relationship. We are not to "corrupt it or confuse it" with distractions that take away from the relationship by diminishing it in importance or value. We are to nurture and care for the primary person in our lives, with mutual self-giving, "out of reverence for Christ" (Eph. 5:21).

Guidelines

Divide into groups of three to five persons to discuss one or two of the following questions. We recommend that you select only one or two questions in order to have a more in-depth discussion. If your group finishes discussing the questions before the allotted time has passed, feel free to move on to another question.

1. Reflect on one of the three commandments discussed. Share how you as a community can work to obey that commandment more fully. Be specific about your ideas.

2. Reflect on the *Study Catechism* questions and answers for this session and share one new thought or understanding that the catechism has offered you.

3. In a culture that demands more and more of you, what can your community of faith do to encourage "right" relationships between men and women? Discuss the types of things that encourage "adulterating" primary relationships in our culture.

4. Why do you believe we should value older parents? How does your community value and celebrate older adults? What can you do to strengthen the way your community upholds this commandment?

5. How does your community deal with anger and conflict? Does it avoid it? deny it? dramatize it? embrace it? How can your community better equip itself in the area of conflict resolution? What kinds of programs or activities could be developed? Think about this issue as it relates to youth; engaged and married couples; extended families; and church meetings.

6. Under what circumstances do you think it is legitimate for a person to *"limit"* their *"obligation to obey"* their father or mother *(SC#106)?* Why do you believe this understanding to be important or relevant today?

CASE STUDIES (20 MINUTES)

Guidelines

Divide the class into groups of three to five persons to read and discuss the following case studies. Assign Case Study #1 to half the groups and Case Study #2 to the other half.

1. Robert and Cindy are two of your closest friends and are also members of your church. Robert and Cindy are young professionals and are both extremely gifted and driven. Their two children, Dakota and Madison, are four and six years of age. Recently you have noticed that Robert and Cindy are rarely seen together. They have refused your last three invitations to do something together as couples. They say they are either working at the office or just "busy." Cindy casually mentioned that there had been a good deal of "tension" at home recently. You and your spouse are concerned by this change of behavior in Robert and Cindy. *What would you do? Why? How would you address the situation? What might you tell Robert and/or Cindy? What are the relevant issues and concerns? What catechism questions and answers or biblical texts seem to be most relevant to this discussion?*

2. Susan's seventy-five-year-old mother, Ann, is not doing well physically. She is showing signs of severe dementia. Ann has lived with Susan and her husband, Brad, for the past decade. Susan and Brad are working full time and trying to put their three children through college. It has become very difficult for them to adequately care for Ann. They are considering putting her in a facility for the elderly, but are not certain that this is the right thing for them to do as Christians. They bring up the topic at your weekly Bible study. *How would you respond? What would you tell them and why? What are the primary issues and concerns? Think about words such as "honor, dignity, love, care" as you discuss their situation in the group. What catechism questions and answers, and which biblical texts seem to be relevant to the discussion?*

CLOSING PRAYER (5 MINUTES)

Stand in a circle for a closing prayer. Invite all in turn to thank God for the person to their left. Keep the prayers short and simple. An example is: "Thank you, God, for [name of person] and the [name a gift] they bring to this community [e.g. insights, wisdom, laughter]." Close together with the Lord's Prayer.

Optional Exercises

These optional exercises may be included as part of the group session following the case-study discussion. Alternatively, class members may use the Questions for Personal Reflection to add to their journaling between classes.

QUESTIONS FOR PERSONAL REFLECTION (20 MINUTES)

Guidelines

Invite the group members to individually and silently reflect on one of these questions. Allow at least ten minutes for this quiet time. Come back together as a group, and invite members to share some of their thoughts. Allow ten minutes for sharing.

1. Which of these three commandments are you currently struggling with? What can you do to make a positive change in your life?

2. In what way(s) are you guilty of "adulterating" your primary relationship? What can you do to work at honoring that relationship?

3. What can you do to better "honor" your father or mother? Or: In what ways would you like your children to "honor" you?

4. Understanding the Sixth Commandment, "You shall not murder" as inclusive of ***"an angry word or a clever plan" (SC#108),*** reflect on a time that you have been guilty of breaking this commandment.

For Further Reading

Barclay, William. *The Ten Commandments.* Louisville, Ky.: Westminster John Knox Press, 1998.

Hauerwas, Stanley, and William H. Willimon. *The Truth about God: The Ten Commandments in Christian Life.* Nashville: Abingdon Press, 1999.

Killinger, John. *To My People with Love: The Ten Commandments for Today.* Nashville: Abingdon Press, 1988. Chapters on the Fifth, Sixth, and Seventh Commandments, pp. 58–90.

Living as a People of Faith in the World

Theme:

This session will continue to focus on furthering our understanding of what it means to be called to respect and cherish our relationships with others, as reflected in the Eighth, Ninth, and Tenth Commandments.

The *Study Catechism*: Questions 111–119

Question 111. What is the eighth commandment?

"You shall not steal" (Ex. 20:15; Deut. 5:19).

Question 112. What do you learn from this commandment?

God forbids all theft and robbery, including schemes, tricks, or systems that unjustly take what belongs to someone else. God requires me not to be driven by greed, not to misuse or waste the gifts I have been given, and not to distrust the promise that God will supply my needs.

Question 113. What is the ninth commandment?

"You shall not bear false witness against your neighbor" (Ex. 20:16; Deut. 5:20).

Question 114. What do you learn from this commandment?

God forbids me to damage the honor or reputation of my neighbor. I should not say false things against anyone for the sake of money, favor, or friendship, for the sake of revenge, or for any other reason. God requires me to speak the truth, to speak well of my neighbor when I can, and to view the faults of my neighbor with tolerance when I cannot.

Question 115. Does this commandment forbid racism and other forms of negative stereotyping?

Yes. In forbidding false witness against my neighbor, God forbids me to be prejudiced against people who belong to any vulnerable, different, or disfavored social group. Jews, women, homosexuals, racial and ethnic minorities, and national enemies are among those who have suffered terribly from being subjected to the slurs of social prejudice. Negative stereotyping is a form of falsehood that invites actions of humiliation, abuse, and violence as forbidden by the commandment against murder.

Question 116. What is the tenth commandment?

"You shall not covet what is your neighbor's" (Ex. 20:17; Deut. 5:21).

Question 117. What do you learn from this commandment?

My whole heart should belong to God alone, not to money or the things of this world. "Coveting" means desiring something wrongfully. I should not resent the good fortune or success of my neighbor or allow envy to corrupt my heart.

Question 118. What is the best summary of the last six commandments?

These teach me how to live rightly with my neighbor. Jesus summed them up with the commandment which is like the greatest one about loving God: "You shall love your neighbor as yourself" (Matt. 22:39; Lev. 19:18).

Question 119. Can you obey these commandments perfectly?

No. I am at once a *forgiven* sinner and a forgiven *sinner.* As a sinner without excuse, I fail to obey these commandments as God requires. "For whoever keeps the whole law but fails in one point has become accountable for all of it" (James 2:10). I should not adjust the law to my failures, nor reduce my failures before God. Yet there is more grace in God than sin in me. While I should not cease to pray to God for mercy, I can be confident that God is forgiving and that I will be set free from all my sins. By grace I can confess my sins, repent of them, and grow in love and knowledge day by day.

Individual Preparation

Read the catechism questions and answers above and then read the Historical and Theological Background section. Suggestions for Keeping a Journal follow this section.

Historical and Theological Background

We shift focus to the final three commandments with this session, but we remain with the questions: How are the faithful children of God to behave with regard to one another? and, What is the appropriate attitude for the children of God in their daily interaction with others? These final three laws emphasize promoting and cherishing life through the preservation of a person's dignity and reputation.

The Eighth Commandment

"You shall not steal." The Eighth Commandment deals with the kind of behavior and spirit that keeps a community healthy and vibrant. We are reminded that *"God forbids all theft and robbery, including schemes, tricks, or systems that unjustly take what belongs to someone else. God requires me not to be driven by greed" (SC#112).* Greed and theft shatter trust and break relationships. Stealing is not limited to material goods. It includes stealing nonmaterial goods, such as a person's reputation or time, without due compensation. A person "steals not only when he robs a man's strongbox or his pocket, but also when he takes advantage of his neighbor."[1] This crime is seen in Jeremiah: "Woe to him who builds his house by unrighteousness,/and his upper rooms by injustice;/who makes his neighbors work for nothing,/and does not give them their wages" (Jer. 22:13).

By its positive implication, this commandment directs us to treat others fairly in all professional or personal affairs. Jesus warned of the danger of greed, claiming that "one's life does not consist in the abundance of possessions" (Luke 12:15). Jesus is our strongest model in this regard. Throughout his life and teaching he was concerned with the welfare of those whose human dignity and material wealth were on the fringe of the disfranchised. As faith members of the covenant community, we are called to live out a commitment to the welfare of others.

The Ninth Commandment

"You shall not bear false witness against your neighbor" focuses on the preservation of a person's reputation and "good name." *God forbids me to damage the honor or reputation of my neighbor. I should not say false things against anyone for the sake of money, favor, or friendship, [or] for the sake of revenge" (SC#114).* Our reputations and "good names" are often the only things that carry us through emotional and financial tough times. When one's name is intentionally and falsely damaged, it can be extremely painful and even devastating. In many ways "honor and good name" can be understood as "indispensable treasures for us . . . , for it is intolerable to live among men in public disgrace and contempt."[2] Lying brings great harm, not only to the individuals involved, but to the community, as it tears into the fabric of basic trust at the core of healthy human relationships.

The positive implication of this commandment directs members of the covenant community to "faithfully help everyone as much as we can in affirming the truth, in order to protect the integrity of his name and possessions."[3] The New Testament Letter of James strongly admonishes members of community, "Do not speak evil against one another" (James 4:11). This commandment requires not only that we speak the truth, but that we become active agents on behalf of those whose voices have been silenced because of economic, physical, or emotional circumstances. Listen to the words of wisdom found in Proverbs: "Speak out for those who cannot speak, for the rights of all the destitute. Speak out, judge righteously, defend the rights of the poor and needy" (Prov. 31:8–9).

The Tenth Commandment

This commandment, "You shall not covet . . . ," should not be understood as the least important of the ten. This commandment addresses a sin that cannot be clearly seen or identified by others. It reminds us that *"My whole heart should belong to God alone, not to money or the things of this world. 'Coveting' means desiring something wrongfully" (SC#117).* When our hearts and minds are compromised with wrongful and selfish desires, all the other commandments are in danger of being broken. In effect, this commandment functions as a kind of "summary commandment, the violation of which is a first step that can lead to the violation of any one or all the rest of the commandments."[4]

If we are not to covet any possessions or people and lives belonging to our neighbor, it naturally follows that we are to "keep [our] lives free from the love of money, and be content with what [we] have" (Heb. 13:5). We are to live with appreciation and a sense of contentment. We are called to live with a spirit of generosity and love. "God wills that our whole soul be possessed with a disposition to love."[5] It is love based on trust and faithfulness to one another and God that helps build the foundation of a covenant community. Coveting compromises the possibility of that love.

"As a sinner without excuse, I fail to obey these commandments as God requires. 'For whoever keeps the whole law but fails in one point has become accountable for all of it' (James 2:10). I should not adjust the law to my failures, nor reduce my failures before God. Yet there is more grace in God than sin in me. While I should not cease to pray to God for mercy, I can be confident that God is forgiving and that I will be set free from all my sins" (SC#119). Our broken and sinful nature makes us incapable of faithfully keeping these commandments. Yet, we must continue striving for Christlike patterns of behavior in all our relationships. We are to persevere, continuing to seek that way of life which truly reflects the grace of Jesus, the Christ, in our lives. "For by grace [we] have been saved through faith, and this is not [our] own doing; it is a gift of God" (Eph. 2:8). *"By grace I can confess my sins, repent of them, and grow in love and knowledge day by day" (SC#119).* And as the catechism says, *"there is more grace in God than sin in me."* This statement serves as encouragement for each of us as we seek to follow Christ.

KEEPING A JOURNAL

1. Continue your personal journal on the Ten Commandments, focusing this week on commandments eight, nine, and ten. At the beginning of each day, recite Psalm 100. At the end of the day, affirm one way in which you have been able to keep these commandments. Confess one way in which you broke these commandments. At the end of the week, reflect and give thanks for the gift of the law. Ask God to help you with areas in which you need growth.

2. Reread the catechism questions and answers for this session. Choose one sentence or phrase to "hang on to" for the week. Here are some ideas:

    *   "God requires me not to be driven by greed, not to misuse or waste the gifts I have been given, and not to distrust the promise that God will supply my needs."

    *   "God requires me to speak the truth, to speak well of my neighbor when I can, and to view the faults of my neighbor with tolerance when I cannot."

    *   "My whole heart should belong to God alone, not to money or the things of this world."

- "Yet there is more grace in God than sin in me."
- "While I should not cease to pray to God for mercy, I can be confident that God is forgiving and that I will be set free from all my sins."

Maybe one of these, or another phrase, is particularly meaningful to you. See if you can memorize it, or at least remember the gist of it. Let this phrase stick with you through the week. Include it in your prayers, think about it while you are in the car, and remember it in the midst of a stressful situation. Look for connections between the phrase you selected and the world around you. Perhaps a conversation, a TV show, a current event, or a situation at home or at work will remind you of it. Record your thoughts and observations about this phrase and others in the journal space provided.

3. Consider using the Questions for Personal Reflection at the end of Session 3 (page 55) to reflect on last week's material if you did not already complete this exercise in class.

Group Session

OPENING PRAYER (5 MINUTES)

Have the group leader or another class member open the session with prayer. Invite those who are willing to share the catechism phrase they focused on in their journaling.

KEY BIBLICAL REFERENCES (15 MINUTES)

Guidelines

Assign individual class members the catechism questions and accompanying scripture passages listed below. Read catechism Questions 111 and 112 responsively, with one person asking the question and the rest of the class reading the answer aloud in unison. (See page 56 for catechism questions.) Have the assigned class member read aloud the corresponding scripture passages. Follow this pattern for Questions 113–119 as well.

a. Eighth Commandment: *Study Catechism* Questions 111–112 (Ex. 20:15; Deut. 5:19)

b. Ninth Commandment: *Study Catechism* Questions 113–115 (Ex. 20:16; Deut. 5:20)

c. Tenth Commandment: *Study Catechism* Questions 116–119 (Ex. 20:17; Deut. 5:21)

OPTIONAL BIBLICAL REFERENCES

Guidelines

These scripture references are provided to expand your understanding. You may want to assign teams to find these and report back when discussing the particular question. Alternatively, you may use these for further study and reflection at home.

a. Eighth Commandment: Jer. 22:13; Luke 12:15; 1 Tim. 6:9–10

b. Ninth Commandment: Zech. 8:16–17; Prov. 31:8–9; James 4:11

c. Tenth Commandment: Heb. 13:5; Matt. 19:21

HISTORICAL AND THEOLOGICAL BACKGROUND (5–10 MINUTES)

You have three options for this section:

1. The teacher may summarize the main points of the material (found on pages 58–60) that was read by class members in preparation for the group session.

2. The teacher may ask for volunteers to share one or two important points they remember from the Historical and Theological Background section.

3. If your group is coming to this session without advance preparation, you may ask several group members to take turns reading aloud the Historical and Theological Background material (found on pages 58–60).

REFLECTIONS FOR CHRISTIANS TODAY (5 MINUTES)

Guidelines

Have several class members take turns reading aloud this section.

In the Eighth Commandment—"You shall not steal"—we are called to respect the possessions and dignity of our neighbor. Stealing is a profound violation of an individual, a household, or a community. It is easy for us to avoid identifying ourselves with this sin. After all, how many of us actually steal anything that doesn't belong to us? The truth is that we often take credit for thoughts and ideas that are not ours. This is a form of stealing. Anything that is an "attack on the dignity of human beings and their work"[6] can be understood as theft. We steal from our neighbors, present and future, when we contribute to the pollution of water or the destruction of natural resources.

This commandment is about more than just preserving our material wealth or the material wealth of others. It reminds us that it is precisely because we are members of a covenant community that we are to work actively toward ensuring that all people have enough to live. We cannot live in isolation, content that we have been blessed. We are to help those who are unable to help themselves. We cannot say we are a people of grace and love if we refuse to participate in lessening the injustices around us. "How does God's love abide in anyone who has the world's goods and sees a brother or sister in need and yet refuses help?" (1 John 3:17). We will be judged as an unloving people, and therefore a godless one. Finally, this commandment reminds us *"not to distrust the promise that God will supply [our] needs" (SC#112)*. It is a call to trust in the Creator of the universe instead of trusting our own personal agendas.

In the Ninth Commandment—"You shall not bear false witness against your neighbor"—we are called to resist the temptation to misrepresent the truth about our neighbor in the world. This is an especially challenging commandment because it forces us to look at how we are often tempted to create false snapshots or stereotypes of others, especially when we are uncomfortable with them. This often happens with people whom we perceive as different because of religion, race, gender, or physical ability. We also sometimes have false perceptions about and bear false witness against people who disagree with us. This commandment forbids the children of God to "malign anyone with slanders or false charges, nor harm his substance by falsehood, in short, injure him by unbridled evil speaking and impudence."[7] We instead are called to reflect a "constant love for one another" (1 Peter 4:8).

In a world where hate crimes are prevalent and places of worship are burned, in a culture where many are still disfranchised because of who they are or what they believe, it is imperative for a people of faith to proclaim the importance of human dignity for each individual. *"In forbidding false witness against my neighbor, God forbids me to be prejudiced against people who belong to any vulnerable, different, or disfavored social group. Jews, women, homosexuals, racial and ethnic minorities, and national enemies are among those who have suffered terribly from being subjected to the slurs of social prejudice. Negative stereotyping is a form of falsehood that invites actions of humiliation, abuse, and violence as forbidden by the commandment against murder"* *(SC#115).* We are called to understand our God-created uniqueness and differences while celebrating the commonality of our humanity. Most importantly, we are called to be active agents, faithfully helping "everyone as much as we can in affirming the truth, in order to protect the integrity of their name and possessions."[8]

In the Tenth Commandment—"You shall not covet what is your neighbor's"—we are called to resist the "Madison Avenue" marketing drive for more possessions. Coveting—or desiring things in an uncontrollable way—is a sin that slowly eats away at our inner self. It causes us to lose perspective on who we are as children of God. It encourages the flawed thinking that our identity is somehow tied to the external object we desire. When that desire takes over our heart, it leads us to the possibility of breaking every other commandment. The object of our desire becomes such that we immediately break the First Commandment, for we have replaced our love of God with the love of a possession. The rest is a domino effect.

In a world where "wanting more" is an underlying value, we are called to be generous of spirit; generous with who we are and what we have. As children of the covenant, we are called to trust God and to believe that God is faithful to God's promise of eternal presence in our lives—"I will never leave you or forsake you" (Heb. 13:5). We must trust God more than all the wealth we can accumulate, and must resist the temptation to create false worlds of security based on money, power, success and the like. At the same time, we are called to be responsible stewards of all we have received—health, money, the people in our lives, our gifts, and the planet, for example. We should *"not resent the good fortune or success of [our] neighbor or allow envy to corrupt [our] heart" (SC#117).* Envy has a way of "breeding discontent, which can easily lead to abuse and crimes in our relationships with others."[9] We are clearly called to combat those forces and to work diligently to destroy "all the roots and causes of our injuries to our neighbors."[10]

QUESTIONS FOR SMALL-GROUP REFLECTION AND DISCUSSION
(20 MINUTES)

Guidelines

Divide into groups of three to five persons to discuss one or two of the following groups of questions. We recommend that you select only one or two questions in order to have a more in-depth discussion. If your group finishes discussing the questions before the allotted time has passed, feel free to move on to another question.

1. Reflect on one of the final three commandments discussed. Share how you as a community can work to obey that commandment more fully. Be specific about your ideas.

2. Reflect on this particular section of the *Study Catechism* questions and answers and share one new thought or understanding that the catechism has offered you.

3. *"God forbids me to be prejudiced against people who belong to any vulnerable, different, or disfavored social group" (SC#115).* In a culture that focuses on "difference" instead of "commonality," what can your community of faith do to encourage healthy relationships between you and people who are different?

4. In what ways do you understand a concept of "stealing" that goes beyond the theft of material possessions? Give examples of "stealing" that can be found in today's culture.

5. *"Not to distrust the promise that God will supply my needs" (SC#112).* How can you as a community work together to help others understand the difference between seeking what we need to live comfortably in life and wanting it all? How do you understand the distinction between these two values? Why is trusting God for our needs sometimes difficult?

6. *"God requires me to speak the truth, to speak well of my neighbor when I can, and to view the faults of my neighbor with tolerance*

when I cannot" (SC#114). What are some of the cultural messages that discourage us from (1) speaking the truth; (2) speaking well of our neighbor; or (3) developing tolerance of someone we do not particularly like?

CASE STUDIES (20 MINUTES)

Guidelines

Divide the class into groups of three to five persons to read and discuss the following case studies. Assign Case Study #1 to half the groups and Case Study #2 to the other half.

1. Dick is a Christian social worker who has been working closely with his supervisor, Judy. Judy has begun to speak ill of a colleague by the name of Jennifer. Recently, it seems that every time Dick and Judy are together, Jennifer's name finds its way into the conversation. The remarks are insulting and cruel. Dick also believes most of the allegations are untrue. He suspects that Judy does not like Jennifer because of her religious background. Jennifer is a Muslim. Dick has been debating whether or not to confront Judy about her statements against Jennifer. He is also debating whether or not he should let Jennifer know what is being said about her. *If you were Dick, what would you do? How would you approach the problem? What are some of the complexities involved? What catechism questions and answers, biblical texts, and commandments seem to be most relevant or helpful to this situation? Why?*

2. Jill and Dan are to all intents and purposes the "all-American" couple. Jill works part-time and takes care of their three children, while Dan works full-time. They are struggling a bit with their finances. In spite of their two incomes, they can't seem to get ahead of all their payments. You belong to a couples group with them. You have recently noticed that, on the one hand, they are complaining about their finances; while on the other hand they continue to buy new things for their home. At a recent gathering they informed the group that they were building an extension to their home. They said it would look bigger and better than the one belonging to their neighbor down the street. You really care for their family, but don't want to interfere or offer advice when not requested. *What issues are Jill and Dan possibly struggling with? What might be contributing to their inability to keep up with their payments? What, if anything, would you say to them? What catechism questions and answers, biblical texts, and commandments seem to be relevant or helpful to this scenario?*

CLOSING PRAYER (5 MINUTES)

Have a class member lead the group in a time of silent prayer. Ask God for the courage and wisdom to obey the commandments.

Optional Exercises

These optional exercises may be included as part of the group session following the case-study discussion. Alternatively, class members may use the Questions for Personal Reflection to add to their journaling between classes.

QUESTIONS FOR PERSONAL REFLECTION (20 MINUTES)

Guidelines

Invite group members to reflect individually and silently on one or more of these questions. Allow at least ten minutes of quiet. Come back together as a group and invite members to share some of their thoughts. Allow ten minutes for sharing.

1. Which of these three commandments are you currently struggling with? Reflect and reread the *Study Catechism* section on that commandment.

2. *"God requires me not to be driven by greed" (SC#112).* When have you been guilty of "greed"? Or: Reflect on a time when you had something stolen from you (material or emotional). What were the circumstances, and what did you experience emotionally?

3. *"God forbids me to damage the honor or reputation of my neighbor" (SC#114).* When have you "born false witness" against another? What can you do to reflect the call to truthfulness that this commandment requires?

4. *"My whole heart should belong to God alone" (SC#117).* What are signs in your life of having a "covetous" attitude? What can you do to be more generous with who you are and what you have?

For Further Reading

Icenogle, Gareth Weldon. *Biblical Foundations for Small Group Ministry: An Integrated Approach.* Downers Grove, Ill.: InterVarsity Press, 1994.

Killinger, John. *To My People with Love.* Nashville: Abingdon Press, 1988. Chapters on the Eighth, Ninth, and Tenth Commandments, pp. 91–121.

SESSION 5

The Gift of Prayer

Theme:

This session will seek to introduce and understand prayer as an essential part of our life as a people of faith. Together we will explore why we pray and understand how God answers our prayers. We will also begin reflecting on the model prayer that Jesus taught his disciples.

The *Study Catechism*: Questions 120–125

Question 120. What is prayer?

Prayer means calling upon God whose Spirit is always present with us. In prayer we approach God with reverence, confidence, and humility. Prayer involves both addressing God in praise, confession, thanksgiving, and supplication, and listening for God's word within our hearts. When we adore God, we are filled with wonder, love, and praise before God's heavenly glory, not least when we find it hidden in the cross of Golgotha. When confessing our guilt to God, we ask for forgiveness with humble and sorry hearts, remembering that God is gracious as well as holy. When giving thanks to God, we acknowledge God's great goodness, rejoicing in God for all that is so wonderfully provided for us. Finally, when calling upon God to hear our requests, we affirm that God draws near in every need and sorrow of life, and ask God to do so again.

Question 121. What is the purpose of prayer?

Prayer brings us into communion with God. The more our lives are rooted in prayer, the more we sense how wonderful

God is in grace, purity, majesty, and love. Prayer means offering our lives completely to God, submitting ourselves to God's will, and waiting faithfully for God's grace. Through prayer God frees us from anxiety, equips us for service, and deepens our faith.

Question 122. *How does God respond to our prayers?*

God takes all our prayers into account, weighing them with divine wisdom, and responding to them by a perfect will. Although for the time being God's answers may seem beyond our understanding, or sometimes even bitter, we know nonetheless that they are always determined by the grace of our Lord Jesus Christ. God answers our prayers, particularly for temporal blessings, only in ways that are compatible with the larger purposes of God's glory and our salvation. Communion with God is finally the answer within the answers to all our prayers.

Question 123. *What encourages us to pray each day?*

The God who has adopted us as children is the God who encourages and commands us to pray. When we pray, we respond with love to that greater love which meets us from above. Before we enter into prayer, God is ready to grant all that we need. We may turn to God with confidence each day, not because we are worthy, but simply because of God's grace. By praying we acknowledge that we depend on grace for all that is good, beautiful, life-giving, and true.

Question 124. *What prayer serves as our rule or pattern?*

Our rule or pattern is found in the Lord's Prayer, which Jesus taught to his disciples:

> Our Father in heaven,
>   hallowed be your name,
> your kingdom come,
> your will be done,
>   on earth as in heaven.
> Give us today our daily bread.
> Forgive us our sins
>   as we forgive those who sin against us.
> Save us from the time of trial
>   and deliver us from evil.
> For the kingdom, the power, and the glory are yours
>   now and for ever. Amen.

These words express everything that we may desire and expect from God.

Question 125. What is the design of the Lord's Prayer?

The Lord's Prayer falls into two parts, preceded by an opening address, and concluded by a "doxology" or word of praise. Each part consists of three petitions. The first part concerns God's glory; the second part, our salvation. The first part involves our love for God; the second part, God's love for us. The petitions in part one will not be fulfilled perfectly until the life to come; those in part two relate more directly to our present needs here and now.

Individual Preparation

Read the catechism questions and answers above and then read the Historical and Theological Background section. Suggestions for Keeping a Journal follow this section.

HISTORICAL AND THEOLOGICAL BACKGROUND

Understanding Prayer

It was almost two thousand years ago when Jesus taught his followers to pray. This was not an uncommon practice among teachers of his time. It was a way of offering their followers something that would be unique among their particular community. Before Jesus, John the Baptist had also taught his disciples to pray (Luke 11:1). Prayer has been understood as a critical component of the relationship between God and humanity. Through prayer, we are called to approach our creator God with "reverence, confidence, and humility" (SC#120). Prayer is where creature meets the Creator. In prayer we realize that "all masks and camouflage may and must fall away."[1] There is no hiding. Prayer is a profound "matter of the heart and spirit, although the tongue may have a part."[2] It is that moment when "we lift our hearts to God alone as the source of our life and our salvation."[3]

The children of God have invoked four primary types of prayers throughout history. The Bible, especially the book of Psalms, contains rich examples of these prayers. Each is a legitimate and important part of the human journey of faith.

1. **Adoration:** *"When we adore God, we are filled with wonder, love, and praise before God's heavenly glory, not least when we find it hidden in the cross of Golgotha" (SC#120).* "Great is the Lord and

greatly to be praised." Psalm 48:1 expresses joy and confidence in God. This prayer proclaims the "otherness" of God, the creator. Such prayers of adoration praise God for faithful love, mighty acts, and gracious compassion.

2. **Confession:** *"When confessing our guilt to God, we ask for forgiveness with humble and sorry hearts, remembering that God is gracious as well as holy" (SC#120).* "If we confess our sins, he who is faithful and just will forgive us our sins and cleanse us from all unrighteousness" (1 John 1:9). Confession represents the painful awareness that we are broken vessels, unworthy to approach the God of creation. But as affirmed in 1 John and the words of the *Study Catechism,* confession also represents a profound trust in the promises of God. We confess our sins to the One who has assured us of forgiveness.

3. **Thanksgiving:** *"When giving thanks to God, we acknowledge God's great goodness, rejoicing in God for all that is so wonderfully provided for us" (SC#120).* "We give thanks to you, O God; we give thanks; your name is near" (Ps. 75:1). This psalm is a simple example of heartfelt thankfulness. Prayers of thanksgiving acknowledge God as the source of all life and blessings.

4. **Supplication:** *"When calling upon God to hear our requests, we affirm that God draws near in every need and sorrow of life, and ask God to do so again" (SC#120).* "To that end keep alert and always persevere in supplication for all the saints" (Eph. 6:18). Prayers of supplication are made on behalf of ourselves and others. When we ask God for healing, compassion, strength, or wisdom in the midst of difficult situations, we are proclaiming that we are certain of God's presence in our lives. We are confident that God listens and will respond to our prayers. This is a hope-filled prayer, for it trusts that God is concerned with our every need.

Purpose of Prayer and God's Response

The ultimate purpose of prayer is to bring us *"into communion with God. The more our lives are rooted in prayer, the more we sense how wonderful God is in grace, purity, majesty, and love. Prayer means offering our lives completely to God, submitting ourselves to God's will, and waiting faithfully for God's grace. Through prayer God frees us from anxiety, equips us for service, and deepens our faith" (SC #121).* In prayer we come face-to-face with our Maker. A life of prayer— both private and communal—strengthens our relationship with God. Prayer deepens our commitment to God, our commitment to be active agents of God's grace in this world; and our faith to wait upon the promises of God.

As we wait upon God's promises, there are times that the assumed or hoped-for response from God does not seem to come. Through faith we affirm that *"God takes all our prayers into account, weighing them with divine wisdom, and responding to them by a perfect will. Although for the time being God's answers may seem beyond our understanding, or sometimes even bitter, we know nonetheless that they are always determined by the grace of our Lord Jesus Christ" (SC#122).* When struggling with what we perceive as "unanswered" prayer, we can take comfort in the actual *"communion with God" (SC#122)* that we experience in prayer. The knowledge that we are in the presence of God gives great inner peace in the midst of life's turmoil.

Our faith in Jesus Christ and our knowledge of God's grace encourages us to pray daily. *"The God who has adopted us as children is the God who encourages and commands us to pray. When we pray, we respond with love to that greater love which meets us from above. Before we enter into prayer, God is ready to grant all that we need" (SC #123).* Our confidence that we have been adopted as children of God encourages us to pray both privately and in community. God's gracious first act opens our hearts to respond with love. Through prayer, we answer God's call. It is always our *response* to God's initiating love. Listen for the words of the Old Testament book of Isaiah: "Before they call I will answer, while they are yet speaking I will hear" (Isa. 65:24). This is the God to whom we pray. It is this awesome and grace-filled God who draws us into communion through prayer.

Our Pattern for Prayer

For centuries, Christians of every color and nationality have learned the prayer that Jesus prayed and taught his disciples. It is a prayer that "we utter as members of the people of God, rather than as isolated individuals."[4] The Lord's Prayer is the model, or rule, for prayer for Christians. The prayer can be divided into two major sections of six petitions. The first three of these petitions are "concerned first and foremost with God and what is owed to God. The second set of three petitions is concerned with human need."[5] These six petitions are framed within an opening address and a closing doxology.

KEEPING A JOURNAL

1. Keep a daily journal of personal prayer. Each day identify the kind of prayer you are writing and why.

2. Reread the catechism questions and answers for this session. Choose one sentence or phrase to "hang on to" for the week. Here are some ideas:

- "When calling upon God to hear our requests, we affirm that God draws near in every need and sorrow of life."
- "The more our lives are rooted in prayer, the more we sense how wonderful God is in grace, purity, majesty, and love."
- "Through prayer God frees us from anxiety, equips us for service, and deepens our faith."
- "Communion with God is finally the answer within the answers to all our prayers."
- "When we pray, we respond with love to that greater love which meets us from above."

Maybe one of these, or another phrase, is particularly meaningful to you. See if you can memorize it, or at least remember the gist of it. Let this phrase stick with you through the week. Include it in your prayers, think about it while you are in the car, and remember it in the midst of a stressful situation. Look for connections between the phrase you selected and the world around you. Perhaps a conversation, a TV show, a current event, or a situation at home or at work will remind you of it. Record your thoughts and observations about this phrase and others in the journal space provided.

3. Consider using the Questions for Personal Reflection at the end of Session 4 (page 69) to reflect on last week's material if you did not already complete this exercise in class.

Group Session

OPENING PRAYER (5 MINUTES)

Have the group leader or another class member open the session with prayer. Invite those who are willing to share the catechism phrase they focused on in their journaling.

KEY BIBLICAL REFERENCES (15 MINUTES)

Guidelines

Assign individual class members the catechism questions and accompanying scripture passages listed below. Read catechism Question 120 responsively, with one person asking the question and the rest of the class reading the answer aloud in unison. (See page 70 for catechism questions.) Have the assigned class member read aloud the corresponding scripture passages. Follow this pattern for Questions 121–125 as well.

a. *Study Catechism* Question 120 (Ps. 48:1; James 5:16; Ps. 75:1; Eph. 6:18)

b. *Study Catechism* Questions 121–123 (Matt. 7:7–8; 1 John 5:14; Isa. 65:24)

c. *Study Catechism* Questions 124–125 (Matt. 6:9–13; Luke 11:2–4)

HISTORICAL AND THEOLOGICAL BACKGROUND (5–10 MINUTES)

You have three options for this section:

1. The teacher may summarize the main points of the material (found on pages 72–74) that was read by class members in preparation for the group session.

2. The teacher may ask for volunteers to share one or two important points they remember from the Historical and Theological Background section.

3. If your group is coming to this session without advance preparation, you may ask several group members to take turns reading aloud the Historical and Theological Background material (found on pages 72–74).

REFLECTIONS FOR CHRISTIANS TODAY (5 MINUTES)

Guidelines

Have several class members take turns reading aloud this section.

It is difficult to maintain the priority of prayer in a culture that does not value time apart and alone. In a "calendar–driven" society, prayer is often mistaken as "doing nothing." Prayer is viewed as passive and unproductive by a society that rewards busyness and activity. The truth about prayer is far different from these popular assumptions.

By the power of the Holy Spirit, prayer equips and prepares us to be ambassadors for Christ in the world. When we go before God with praise, confession, thanksgiving, and supplication, we are brought into the very presence of God. Through prayer we become encouraged; we are given wisdom, and we are strengthened to be the faithful people of God. Prayer summons us "not to passivity but to activity, not to bondage but to freedom, not to indifference about evil in and around us, but to passion for justice, freedom and peace in the whole creation."[6] Karl Barth once said, "To fold one's hands in prayer is the beginning of an uprising against the disorder of the world."[7] This reality offers profound power and hope to the community of the faithful.

The truth is we are not the community of the faithful without prayer. We are but a human community, ill equipped to address the challenges and temptations of this life. Without prayer, we are like empty vessels, disconnected from our source. Our need for prayer is basic to our existence.

QUESTIONS FOR SMALL-GROUP REFLECTION AND DISCUSSION (20 MINUTES)

Guidelines

Divide into groups of three to five persons to discuss one or two of the following groups of questions. We recommend that you select only one or two questions in order to have a more in-depth discussion. If your group finishes discussing the questions before the allotted time has passed, feel free to move on to another question.

1. Select one kind of prayer (adoration, confession, thanksgiving, or supplication). Write a two-to-four-line prayer. Share your written prayer with the members of the group. Explain why you chose that particular prayer type. Refer to catechism Question 120 for direction.

2. When and how does your community pray together? Share one way that your community could strengthen your life of prayer together.

3. In what ways has your community experienced prayer as equipping and active? Be specific. Reflect on actual occasions when you

felt prayer provided your community with the wisdom and courage to act.

4. In the catechism we read, *"Before we enter into prayer, God is ready to grant all that we need" (SC#123).* In what ways has this catechism claim been a reality in your life? What (if anything) about this catechism claim do you struggle with?

5. The catechism affirms that *"Prayer means offering our lives completely to God, submitting ourselves to God's will, and waiting faithfully for God's grace" (SC#121).* How do you feel about this affirmation? What about it can you celebrate? What about it makes you uncomfortable?

6. The catechism affirms that *"Through prayer God frees us from anxiety, equips us for service, and deepens our faith" (SC#121).* What about prayer have you experienced as making you less anxious; more equipped for service; deeper in faith? Share examples of each.

CASE STUDIES (20 MINUTES)

Guidelines

Divide the class into groups of three to five persons to read and discuss the following case studies. Assign Case Study #1 to half the groups and Case Study #2 to the other half.

1. You just learned that your friends Faith and James lost the child they were expecting. Faith was taken to the hospital last night, where she gave birth prematurely. The little girl had no chance of survival. You are going to visit them tomorrow at the hospital. You've heard that they are both emotionally devastated and angry with God. They are wondering where God is in this world. They had been faithfully praying for this child for more than three years. *How will you prepare yourself to visit them? Where will you look for guidance? What will you tell them? What words would you pray with them? What catechism questions and answers and biblical texts seem to be the most helpful and relevant to this situation?*

2. First Presbyterian Church, Anytown, U.S.A., is looking for a new senior pastor. The Pastor Nominating Committee is struggling with its task. The members are unable to create a consensus about the kind of person they're looking for. They seem to be evenly divided into two factions, representing diverse views about the direction the church should be going in the future. They have been working at it and arguing for more than a year. Some members of the committee believe the church needs more prayer. They believe that they

haven't called a pastor because the church has not prayed enough. Others are uncomfortable with what they perceive as "spiritual coercion." Both factions are tired, and their tension is beginning to be felt by the congregation. *You have just been named the new chair of the committee.* A final candidate is coming to visit with the committee in two weeks. You are concerned that the climate of the committee is not favorable for an interview with anyone. You have decided to call a special meeting of the committee to prepare them for meeting with this candidate. *How would you prepare yourself for this meeting? What would you want to tell them? How can you offer a time of prayer in a way that builds community (and not suspicion)? What questions and answers of the catechism and biblical texts do you find most helpful and relevant?*

CLOSING PRAYER (5 MINUTES)

Close with a "popcorn prayer." Class members may offer brief prayers as they feel led. After a time, the teacher may close by leading the group in the Lord's Prayer.

Optional Exercises

These optional exercises may be included as part of the group session following the case-study discussion. Alternatively, class members may use the Questions for Personal Reflection to add to their journaling between classes.

QUESTIONS FOR PERSONAL REFLECTION (20 MINUTES)

Guidelines

Invite group members to reflect individually and silently on one or more of these questions. Allow at least ten minutes of quiet. Come back together as a group and invite members to share some of their thoughts. Allow ten minutes for sharing.

1. Reflect on catechism questions and answers 120 and 121. On a scale of 1 to 5 (5 being the highest), how would you rate your personal prayer life? In what ways can you strengthen habits of prayer in your daily life?

2. In what ways (if any) have you bought into the popular assumption that prayer is passive or inactive?

3. In the catechism we read, *"Although for the time being God's answers may seem beyond our understanding, or sometimes even bitter, we*

know nonetheless that they are always determined by the grace of our Lord Jesus Christ" (SC#122). How do you cope when it is not clear that God is answering your prayer? In what ways is the waiting difficult for you? Where do you find comfort during those times?

4. What do you appreciate about prayer? What about prayer (public or private) makes you uncomfortable? Discuss why.

5. Identify people with whom you are comfortable praying. Thank God for their presence in your life.

MUSICAL EXPRESSION

Bring in a recording of "The Lord's Prayer" set to music. Listen to it at the beginning and at the end of the session. Silently reflect on the words of the prayer as they are sung to music.

For Further Reading

Allen, Diogenes. "What Is Spiritual Theology?" "The Journey and the Goal," and "Contemplation." Chapters 1, 2, and 7 in *Spiritual Theology: The Theology of Yesterday for Spiritual Help Today.* Boston: Cowley Publications, 1997.

Fosdick, Harry Emerson. *The Meaning of Prayer.* New York: Association Press, 1949.

Foster, Richard J. *Prayer: Finding the Heart's True Home.* New York: HarperCollins Publishers, 1992.

Hybels, Bill. *Too Busy Not to Pray: Slowing Down to Be with God.* Downers Grove, Ill.: InterVarsity Press, 1988.

Killinger, John. *Beginning Prayer.* Nashville: Upper Room Books, 1993.

Loder, Ted. *Guerrillas of Grace: Prayers for the Battle.* San Diego: LuraMedia, 1984.

Ramey, Robert H., Jr., and Ben Campbell Johnson. "Prayer as a Means of Grace." Chapter 4 in *Living the Christian Life: A Guide to Reformed Spirituality.* Louisville, Ky.: Westminster/John Knox Press, 1992.

Rice, Howard L. and Lamar Williamson, Jr., editors. "How Reformed Christians Pray." Introduction in *A Book of Reformed Prayers.* Louisville, Ky.: Westminster/John Knox Press, 1998.

Thompson, Marjorie J. "Communication and Communion with God." Chapter 3 in *Soul Feast: An Invitation to the Christian Spiritual Life.* Louisville, Ky.: Westminster/John Knox Press, 1995.

Weems, Ann. *Psalms of Lament.* Louisville, Ky.: Westminster/John Knox Press, 1995.

SESSION 6

Seeking to Be in Communion with God

Theme:

This session will reflect on the Lord's Prayer. We will seek to deepen our understanding of the opening address and the first three petitions as reflected in Questions 126 through 129 of the *Study Catechism.*

The *Study Catechism:* Questions 126–129

Question 126. What is meant by addressing God as "Our Father in heaven"?

By addressing God as "our Father," we draw near with child-like reverence and place ourselves securely in God's hands. Although God is certainly everywhere, God is said to exist and dwell "in heaven." For while God is free to enter into the closest relationship with the creature, God does not belong to the order of created beings. "Heaven" is the seat of divine authority, the place from which God reigns in glory and brings salvation to earth. Our opening address expresses our confidence that we rest securely in God's intimate care and that nothing on earth lies beyond the reach of God's grace.

Question 127. What is meant by the first petition, "Hallowed be your name"?

This petition is placed first, because it comprehends the goal and purpose of the whole prayer. The glory of God's name is the highest concern in all that we pray and do. God's "name" stands for God's being as well as for God's attributes and works. When we pray for this name to be "hallowed," we ask that we and all others will know and glorify God as God really is, and that all things will be so ordered that they serve God truly for God's sake.

Question 128. What is meant by the second petition, "Your kingdom come"?

We are asking God to come and rule among us through faith, love, and justice—and not through any one of them without the others. We pray for both the church and the world, that God will rule in our hearts through faith, in our personal relationships through love, and in our institutional affairs through justice. We ask especially that the gospel will not be withheld from us, but rightly preached and received. We pray that the church will be upheld and increase, particularly when in distress; and that all the world will more and more submit to God's reign, until that day when crying and pain are no more, and we live forever with God in perfect peace.

Question 129. What is meant by the third petition, "Your will be done, on earth as in heaven"?

Of course, God's will is always done and will surely come to pass, whether we desire it or not. But the phrase "on earth as in heaven" means that we ask for the grace to do God's will on earth in the *way* that it is done in heaven—gladly and from the heart. We thus ask that all opposition to God's will might be removed from the earth, and especially from our own hearts. We ask for the freedom to conform our desires and deeds more fully to God's, so that we might be completely delivered from our sin. We yield ourselves, in life and in death, to God's will.

Individual Preparation

Read the catechism questions and answers above and then read the Historical and Theological Background section. Suggestions for Keeping a Journal follow this section.

HISTORICAL AND THEOLOGICAL BACKGROUND

The *Study Catechism* uses the ecumenical version of the Lord's Prayer. This particular version of the Lord's Prayer might feel new or even strange for some. It was chosen as a vote for the future, as churches across the denominations are increasingly turning to this ecumenical version of the Lord's Prayer. In many ways it is an intentional celebration of a uniting factor in contemporary Christendom. Christians of all traditions are in fact united in their one proclamation of Jesus Christ as Lord and Savior. It is this same Jesus who taught us to pray using these precious words.

Opening Address—To Whom Do We Pray, "Our Father in Heaven"?

As we seek to be in communion with God, we are invited into intimate relationship. ***"By addressing God as 'our Father,' we draw near with childlike reverence and place ourselves securely in God's hands" (SC#126).*** "The word 'father' reflects a personal relationship with a personal God. We are able to approach the very God of creation in trust and faith because we believe that 'in Christ we have the privilege of becoming the children of God.'[1] In Romans 8:15–16 we read, "For you did not receive a spirit of slavery to fall back into fear, but you have received a spirit of adoption. When we cry, 'Abba! Father!' it is that very Spirit bearing witness with our spirit that we are children of God."

"We" are the children of God—not "I" in isolation. Even though this prayer was probably taught specifically for the private prayer of the disciples, prayer was not considered a private or individualistic exercise. "The emphasis on 'Our' makes prayer common because the object (God) is the shared good of all."[2] The Lord's Prayer is embraced as the model for prayer. As such, it is a reminder that whenever we approach God in prayer, we are called to do so with an awareness and concern not only for ourselves, but for all of God's children. We do not have the privilege of living safely in isolation. On the contrary, as Christians we are commanded to go forth into the world.

And where in the world can we find God? The opening address of the Lord's Prayer identifies God as being in "heaven." ***"Although God is certainly everywhere, God is said to exist and dwell 'in heaven.' For while God is free to enter into the closest relationship with the creature, God does not belong to the order of created beings" (SC#126).*** In the words of this prayer, Jesus clearly identifies the place of God as "heaven." Heaven is that untainted and sinless place and space; ***"the seat of divine authority, the place from which God reigns in glory and brings salvation to earth" (SC#126).*** We open our prayer with ***"confidence that we rest securely in God's intimate care and that nothing on earth lies beyond the reach of God's grace" (SC#126).***

First Petition: "Hallowed Be Your Name"

"This petition is placed first, because it comprehends the goal and purpose of the whole prayer. The glory of God's name is the highest

concern in all that we pray and do" (SC#127). In thanksgiving and praise we approach God for who God has faithfully been and continues to be in human history. Throughout biblical history, God's name was so revered by the children of Israel that it was not spoken. No one person was considered worthy of invoking God's name. Names were extremely meaningful prior to and during the time of Jesus' ministry on earth. A person's name represented more than a means of identity; it represented a person's character and reputation. A name was intimately related to the "being" of that person. So when we pray, "Hallowed be your name," *"we ask that we and all others will know and glorify God as God really is and that all things will be so ordered that they serve God truly for God's sake" (SC#127).* When we pray these words, we are reminded of the reverence and respect required of us as we dare to approach God. We are reminded that we should "remove the sandals from [our] feet, for the place on which [we] are standing is holy ground" (Ex. 3:5).

Second Petition: "Your Kingdom Come"

When we pray for God's kingdom to come, *"we are asking God to come and rule among us through faith, love, and justice—and not through any one of them without the others. We pray for both the church and the world, that God will rule in our hearts through faith, in our personal relationships through love, and in our institutional affairs through justice" (SC#128).* We acknowledge that the ways of our Creator are the ways that will ultimately save all creation. We relinquish our own earthly mini-kingdoms so that we might allow God's Spirit to enter our lives and lead us. When we pray these words, we are asking that "God's kingdom may prevail 'in us or for us,' in our personal lives."[3] We submit our hopes and dreams, our personal relationships, and our daily decisions to God.

We also pray that the grace and love of Jesus Christ will be experienced and known throughout the world. *"We ask especially that the gospel will not be withheld from us, but rightly preached and received. We pray that the church will be upheld and increase, particularly when in distress; and that all the world will more and more submit to God's reign, until that day when crying and pain are no more, and we live forever with God in perfect peace" (SC#128).* The words to the community of faith in Thessalonica reflect this prayer: "Brothers and sisters, pray for us, so that the word of the Lord may spread rapidly and be glorified everywhere, just as it is among you" (2 Thess. 3:1).

Third Petition: "Your Will Be Done, on Earth as in Heaven"

"Father, if you are willing, remove this cup from me; yet, not my will but yours be done" (Luke 22:42). These well-known words of Jesus, spoken as he faced death, are an acknowledgment that God's will is not always easy. God's will is not always what we desire or understand. At the same time, these words also serve as an acknowledgment that what God ordains and desires will ultimately prevail. At this critical moment in his life, in fear and anguish, Jesus prayerfully accepts the will of God.

"Of course, God's will is always done and will surely come to pass, whether we desire it or not" (SC#129). The truth is that the will of God remains a great mystery for believers. It is often difficult for us to discern God's will. One thing we do know: it is clear throughout scripture that God's will does not reflect the value systems of this world. God's will does not reflect the power structures of society. Paul's wisdom to the Romans reminds us of this reality: "Do not be conformed to this world, but be transformed by the renewing of your minds, so that you may discern what is the will of God—what is good and acceptable and perfect" (Rom. 12:2).

When we pray the words "on earth as in heaven," we are proclaiming the signs of God in our midst. **We ask for the grace to do God's will on earth in the way that it is done in heaven—gladly and from the heart. We thus ask that all opposition to God's will might be removed from the earth, and especially from our own hearts. We ask for the freedom to conform our desires and deeds more fully to God's, so that we might be completely delivered from our sin. We yield ourselves, in life and in death, to God's will" (SC#129).** We are asking that God's perfect love in heaven be the love and grace reflected on earth. We are praying that God's goodness might be reflected in the choices we make and in our relationships with others. We acknowledge that we need God's Holy Spirit within us so that we might be vessels of love and grace, as we seek to be ambassadors of God's love on this earth.

KEEPING A JOURNAL

1. Keep a daily journal of personal prayer. Each day identify the kind of prayer you are writing and why.

2. Reread the catechism questions and answers for this session. Choose one sentence or phrase to "hang on to" for the week. Here are some ideas:

- "Our opening address expresses our confidence that we rest securely in God's intimate care and that nothing on earth lies beyond the reach of God's grace."
- "We pray that the church will be upheld and increase, particularly when in distress."
- ". . . until that day when crying and pain are no more, and we live forever with God in perfect peace."
- "We yield ourselves, in life and in death, to God's will."

Maybe one of these, or another phrase, is particularly meaningful to you. See if you can memorize it, or at least remember the gist of it. Let this phrase stick with you through the week. Include it in your prayers, think about it while you are in the car, and remember it in the midst of a stressful situation. Look for connections between the phrase you selected and the world around you. Perhaps a conversation, a TV show, a current event, or a situation at home or at work will remind you of it. Record your thoughts and observations about this phrase and others in the journal space provided.

3. Consider using the Questions for Personal Reflection at the end of Session 5 (pages 81–82) to reflect on last week's material if you did not already complete this exercise in class.

Group Session

OPENING PRAYER (5 MINUTES)

Have the group leader or another class member open the session with prayer. Invite those who are willing to share the catechism phrase they focused on in their journaling.

KEY BIBLICAL REFERENCES (15 MINUTES)

Guidelines

Assign individual class members the catechism questions and accompanying scripture passages listed below. Read catechism Question 126 responsively, with one person asking the question and the rest of the class reading the answer aloud in unison. (See page 83 above for catechism questions.) Have the assigned class member read aloud the corresponding scripture passages. Follow this pattern for Questions 127–129 as well.

a. *Study Catechism* Question 126 (Matt. 6:9; Luke 11:2; Jer. 23:23–24; Rom. 8:15)

b. *Study Catechism* Question 127 (Matt 6:10; Luke 11:2; Rom. 11:36; Ps. 115:1)

c. *Study Catechism* Question 128 (Matt. 6:20; Luke 11:2; Rev. 22:20; 2 Thess. 3:1)

d. *Study Catechism* Question 129 (Matt. 6:10; Luke 22:42; Ps. 119:34–36)

HISTORICAL AND THEOLOGICAL BACKGROUND (5–10 MINUTES)

You have three options for this section:

1. The teacher may summarize the main points of the material (found on pages 84–87) that was read by class members in preparation for the group session.

2. The teacher may ask for volunteers to share one or two important points they remember from the Historical and Theological Background section.

3. If your group is coming to this session without advance preparation, you may ask several group members to take turns reading the Historical and Theological Background material aloud (found on pages 84–87).

REFLECTIONS FOR CHRISTIANS TODAY (5 MINUTES)

Guidelines

Have several class members take turns reading aloud this section.

There is no doubt that the words of the Lord's Prayer are among the most recognized and repeated words throughout the Christian world. How often have those at the threshold of death been comforted by the sound of these words? How often have those in trouble found courage in the strength of these words? Notwithstanding their familiarity, they have never lost their power and truth for believers of all time.

As a new generation of adults enters the doors of our churches, it is becoming evident that more and more of them are unfamiliar with scripture and the traditions of the church. Many did not grow up attending church. As disciples of the one Jesus, we are called upon to teach these new brothers and sisters, along with the children and youth of the church, the basics of what we believe and how we live as Christians. Among the most basic of Christian practices is prayer, and the most basic and comprehensive prayer is the one that our Lord taught his disciples of yesterday and today to pray.

In the first twenty words of this prayer, we proclaim the reverence and awe that we as creatures are called to have for our Creator. We profess our willingness to allow the Spirit of God to work with and through us. These are necessary elements to all our prayers. And pray we must! Prayer "stands before the innermost centre of the covenant between God and [humanity] which is the meaning and inner basis of creation."[4] Prayer is not an option for the people of Jesus Christ. It is the lifeblood of our relationship with God.

QUESTIONS FOR SMALL-GROUP REFLECTION AND DISCUSSION
(20 MINUTES)

Guidelines

Divide into groups of three to five persons to discuss one or two of the following groups of questions. We recommend that you select only one or two questions in order to have a more in-depth discussion. If your group finishes discussing the questions before the allotted time has passed, feel free to move on to another question.

1. Select one of the first three petitions (or the opening address) in the Lord's Prayer. Read the relevant *Study Catechism* section (Questions 126–129). Share why you selected that phrase and what it means to you.

2. **"We pray for both the church and the world, that God will rule in our hearts through faith, in our personal relationships through love, and in our institutional affairs through justice" (SC#128).** Discuss some ways in which God's rule is evident in the hearts, personal relationships, and institutional affairs of your congregation.

As leaders in your congregation, what are some ways that you can help to foster God's rule in the lives of its members?

3. *"God's 'name' stands for God's being as well as for God's attributes and works" (SC#127).* Discuss the various attributes and works of God that reflect who God is.

4. *"We thus ask that all opposition to God's will might be removed from the earth, and especially from our own hearts" (SC#129).* Reflect on any cultural phenomena, values or activities you believe are against God's will.

5. *"We pray that the church will be upheld and increase, particularly when in distress" (SC#128).* What is your church doing to proclaim the gospel of Jesus Christ beyond the walls of your sanctuary? Celebrate those things. Reflect on what other things can be done.

CASE STUDY (20 MINUTES)

Guidelines

In groups of three to five persons, read the following case study and discuss the questions for fifteen minutes. Share answers with the whole group in the last five minutes.

Lori and Ethan are in your new members' class. They come from a church tradition that focused on the wrath and angry judgment of God. They grew up "fearing God." The notion of "grace" had little to do with their identity as Christians. You are meeting with them as part of the process for receiving them into membership. *How would you distinguish for them the difference between a "God who gets angry" and an "angry God"? Using the catechism Questions 126–129 along with the biblical references, what would you tell them about God?*

CLOSING PRAYER (5 MINUTES)

As a group, recite the words of the Lord's Prayer that you studied today. Have each person do one line: (1) *Our Father in heaven;* (2) *Hallowed be your name;* (3) *Your kingdom come;* (4) *Your will be done, on earth as in heaven.* Keep going until everyone has had a turn.

Optional Exercises

These optional exercises may be included as part of the group session following the case-study discussion. Alternatively, class members may use the Questions for Personal Reflection to add to their journaling during their time between classes.

Guidelines

Invite group members to reflect individually and silently on one or more of these questions. Allow at least ten minutes of quiet. Come back together as a group and invite members to share some of their thoughts. Allow ten minutes for sharing.

1. Reflect on one characteristic of God that you deeply value. In what way do the words "Our Father" reflect (or not reflect) that characteristic?

2. What do you value most about being invited into prayer with God?

3. When proclaiming, "Your kingdom come," we are *". . . asking God to come and rule among us through faith, love, and justice — and not through any one of them without the others" (SC#128)*. What does "God's kingdom" mean to you? What images or words come into your mind when you think of God's rule here on earth?

4. Reflect on a time when it has been difficult for you to say sincerely to God, "Your will be done."

5. *"By addressing God as 'our Father,' we draw near with childlike reverence and place ourselves securely in God's hands" (SC#126)*. Reflect on a time when you approached God in prayer with "childlike reverence" and were able to place yourself in God's hands.

MUSICAL EXPRESSION (20 MINUTES)

Listen to several recordings of "The Lord's Prayer." Discuss how you believe the music enhances (or doesn't enhance) the prayer.

For Further Reading

Bondi, Roberta. Chapters 1–3 in *A Place to Pray: Reflections on the Lord's Prayer*. Nashville: Abingdon Press, 1998.

Willimon, William H., and Stanley Hauerwas. *Lord Teach Us: The Lord's Prayer & the Christian Life*. Nashville: Abingdon Press, 1996.

Migliorie, Daniel L., editor. *The Lord's Prayer: Perspectives for Reclaiming Christian Prayer*. Grand Rapids, Mi: Wm. B. Eerdmans Publishing Company, 1993.

Wright, N.T. Prologue and Chapters 1 and 2 in *The Lord & His Prayer*. Grand Rapids, Mi: Wm. B. Eerdmans Publishing Company; Cincinnati, Oh: Forward Movement Publications, 1996.

Deepening Our Devotion to God

Theme:

The focus of this lesson is deepening our devotion to God through the last three petitions of the Lord's Prayer.

The *Study Catechism:* Questions 130–132

Question 130. What is meant by the fourth petition, "Give us today our daily bread"?

We ask God to provide for all our needs, for we know that God, who cares for us in every area of our life, has promised us temporal as well as spiritual blessings. God commands us to pray each day for all that we need and no more, so that we will learn to rely completely on God. We pray that we will use what we are given wisely, remembering especially the poor and the needy. Along with every living creature we look to God, the source of all generosity, to bless us and nourish us, according to the divine good pleasure.

Question 131. What is meant by the fifth petition, "Forgive us our sins as we forgive those who sin against us"?

We pray that a new and right spirit will be put within us. We ask for the grace to treat others, especially those who harm us, with the same mercy that we have received from God. We remember that not one day goes by when we do not need to turn humbly to God for our own forgiveness. We know that our reception of this forgiveness can be blocked by our unwillingness to forgive others. We ask that we will not delight in doing evil, nor in avenging any wrong, but that we will survive all cruelty without bitterness and overcome evil with good, so that our hearts will be knit together with the mercy and forgiveness of God.

Question 132. What is meant by the final petition, "Save us from the time of trial and deliver us from evil"?

We ask God to protect us from our own worst impulses and from all external powers of destruction in the world. We ask that we might not yield to despair in the face of seemingly hopeless circumstances. We pray for the grace to remember and believe, despite our unbelief, that no matter how bleak the world may sometimes seem, there is nonetheless a depth of love which is deeper than our despair, and that this love—which delivered Israel from slavery in Egypt and raised our Lord Jesus from the dead—will finally swallow up forever all that would now seem to defeat it.

Individual Preparation

Read the catechism questions and answers above and then read the Historical and Theological Background section. Suggestions for Keeping a Journal follow this section.

HISTORICAL AND THEOLOGICAL BACKGROUND

The Lord's Prayer is divided into two nearly symmetrical parts. The first three petitions all include the word "your" while the last three petitions use the word "our" or "us." Similar to the commandments, the first table of the prayer has to do with our love for God and honoring God as God. The second table is about God's love for us in meeting our physical and spiritual needs. While the theological concerns of the first half of the Lord's Prayer are principal and real, the human concerns of the second half will never be "merely secondary or peripheral."[1] The graciousness of God is abundantly seen in Jesus' instruction to pray to 'give us,' 'forgive us,' and 'deliver us.'"

Fourth Petition: "Give Us Today Our Daily Bread"

The request for daily sustenance shows that even our most ordinary needs are of concern to God. In the first instance, the petition is a plea for physical nourishment. Just as the Israelites wandering in the wilderness cried out for food, we lift our voices today. As God provided manna in the wilderness (Exodus 16), so too God desires to grant our prayer for daily sustenance.

The petition is not just a simple prayer for food, however. The Reformed tradition has understood this brief petition for daily bread to be like a doorway to a wider world of concern for our temporal condition. Luther exhorts believers to "enlarge and extend [their] thoughts to include not only the oven or the flour bin, but also the broad fields and the whole land which produce and provide for us our daily bread."[2] Similarly, Calvin asserts that by praying this petition we ask of God "not only for food and clothing but also for everything God perceives to be beneficial to us, that we may eat our daily bread in peace."[3] Thus, this little petition is broad enough to encompass the entire sociopolitical arena, including the stability of the government, "for chiefly through [the civil authorities] does God provide us our daily bread and all the comforts of this life."[4]

For the Reformers, it is not only the needs of the body that are addressed in the fourth petition. We are reminded that when we pray "Give us today our daily bread" we *"ask God to provide for all our needs, for we know that God, who cares for us in every area of our life, has promised us temporal as well as spiritual blessings" (SC#130).* Calvin observes that once we have trusted God for the temporal life and its necessities, we are more ready and able to trust God for the gift of salvation. "Every good and perfect gift comes from above," we read in the letter of James (James 1:17). God's goodness is extended to us body and soul, materially and spiritually. God's grace covers all of life.

Even so, the Reformed tradition cautions against greed and gluttony when praying this petition. Calvin offers an especially sharp word of warning that "those who, not content with daily bread but panting after countless things with unbridled desire, or sated with their abundance, or carefree in their piled-up riches, supplicate God with this prayer are but mocking [God]."[5] The Reformed virtue of simplicity reminds us to *"pray each day for all that we need and no more, . . . that we will use what we are given wisely, remembering especially the poor and the needy" (SC#130).* The form of the petition helps us move beyond the isolation of individual concern into the wider community of humanity. We pray "Give *us* today *our* daily bread" not "Give *me* today *my* daily bread." We are confronted by the unmistakable social implications of the prayer in its plural form. The little word "our" challenges any attempt to privatize the Lord's Prayer.

Fifth Petition: "Forgive Us Our Sins As We Forgive Those Who Sin Against Us"

"Give" and "forgive" are humanity's two great pleas to God. We pray first for food, then for forgiveness, and finally for guidance. God is concerned with our physical needs and our spiritual needs. We pray first for our physical needs to be met so we can live like humans, then for forgiveness for those things we do or have failed to do, in order—as spiritual beings—to live free of guilt and shame.

Calvin's commentary on the fifth petition highlights the Protestant themes of the sinfulness of all people, the universal need for forgiveness, and that forgiveness is given only by the free, unmerited mercy of God. Since Christ is the one commanding us to pray for forgiveness throughout our life, those who believe they have no need of repentance or who hold to a doctrine of "perfect innocence" are defying God. Calvin says, "It pleases God gradually to restore [God's] image in us, in such a manner that some taint always remains in our flesh."[6] Hence, *"we remember that not one day goes by when we do not need to turn humbly to God for our own forgiveness" (SC#131).* There is no place for bargaining with God, since we owe the penalty for our sins. Only God's gracious gift can give us freedom from our sins, accepting us for Christ's sake as if we were innocent.[7]

Luther provides a reason for focusing on the first part of the fifth petition that is both practical and pastoral. With Calvin, he affirms the daily struggle with sin that confronts the baptized. Knowing ourselves and our particular sins of omission and commission, we are prone to lose the "comfort and confidence of the Gospel" as our "conscious becomes restless . . . fear[ing] God's wrath and displeasure." Thus, the daily recitation of this petition provides "the comfort that will restore our conscience."[8] This restoration leads to a properly restored relationship with God marked by our humility and broken pride.

The second part of the petition, "as we forgive those who sin against us," moves us to the ethical plane where we live out the power of being forgiven by God. As the Confession of 1967 reminds us, "to be reconciled to God is to be sent into the world as [God's] reconciling community."[9] This petition connects asking for forgiveness with giving forgiveness. As we have received mercy, so we are to show mercy to others. *"We ask for the grace to treat others, especially those who harm us, with the same mercy that we have received from God" (SC#131).* We do not oblige God to forgive us by forgiving others; God's grace is not something we can earn. However, *"we know that our reception of this forgiveness can be blocked by our unwillingness to forgive others" (SC #131).* The Lord's Prayer bids us to cast out bitterness and desire for revenge and to forgive others out of gratitude for the great mercy shown to us. Thus, *"we ask that we will not delight in doing evil, nor in avenging any wrong, but that we will survive all cruelty without bitterness and overcome evil with good, so that our hearts will be knit together with the mercy and forgiveness of God" (SC#131).*

The Sixth Petition: "Save Us from the Time of Trial and Deliver Us from Evil"

The final petition of the Lord's Prayer is a realistic acknowledgment that we are in the midst of the struggle and that "our striving would be losing"[10] were it not for the power of the One to whom we pray and on whom we rely. Karl Barth observes that "here we are concerned with the great testing . . . the infinitely dangerous threat of that nothingness that is opposed to God."[11] This evil that is in opposition to God is manifested in our world in forms we all recognize—sin and death. Praying this petition, then, is a request *"that we might not yield to despair in the face of seemingly hopeless circumstances" (SC#132).*

The sixth petition looks to the Christian life with a realistic eye. It remembers that "the spirit indeed is willing, but the flesh is weak" (Matt. 26:41). With the apostle, it affirms our human condition: "For I know that nothing good dwells within me, that is, in my flesh. I can will what is right, but I cannot do it. For I do not do the good I want, but the evil I do not want is what I do" (Rom. 7:18–19). The hymn sings: "Sustain us by Thy faith and by Thy power,/And give us strength in every trying hour."[12] When we pray "save us" and "deliver us," we are *"ask[ing] God to protect us from our own worst impulses" (SC#132).*

The word usually translated as "deliver" or "save" can also be translated as "snatch" us from the jaws of the lion's mouth. In the pastoral epistle that bears his name, Peter cautions believers to keep alert, because "like a roaring lion your adversary the devil prowls around, looking for someone to devour" (1 Peter 5:8). The Psalter is filled with the cry to God, "Deliver us," and Christianity echoes this cry in the sixth petition. Christ has unmasked the sinister wickedness of the enemy, and in so doing allows us to call out to God to protect us *"from all external powers of destruction in the world" (SC#132).* We are confident that God will indeed protect us, for, as the Heidelberg Catechism affirms, Jesus Christ "at the cost of his own blood has fully paid for all [our] sins and has completely freed [us] from the dominion of the devil."[13]

Barth is quick to observe that "this last petition also presupposes that we know, more certainly than we know anything else about this danger, that God has already done what we ask of him."[14] That is, in the death and resurrection of Christ, God has triumphed over evil and established the kingdom of God that Christ came proclaiming in his life and ministry. The Confession of 1967 puts it this way:

> Biblical visions and images of the rule of Christ such as a heavenly city, a father's house, a new heaven and earth, a marriage feast, and an unending day culminate in the image of the kingdom. The kingdom represents the triumph of God over all that resists [God's] will and disrupts [God's] creation. Already God's reign is present as a ferment in the world, stirring hope in [people] and preparing the world to receive its ultimate judgment and redemption.[15]

The sixth petition of the Lord's Prayer knows we live in this "in-between time," a time that has "already" arrived, but which is "not yet" fully realized. But it also knows that God's will and way is invincible and the triumph of the kingdom of grace is sure. So we pray *"for the grace to remember and believe, despite our unbelief, that no matter how bleak the world may sometimes seem, there is nonetheless a depth of love which is deeper than our despair, and that this love . . . will finally swallow up forever all that would now seem to defeat it"* (SC#132).

KEEPING A JOURNAL

1. Continue using your prayer journal each day, and throughout this week focus on the three petitions: "give," "forgive," and "deliver." What issues or themes continue to surface?

2. Reread the catechism questions and answers for this session. Choose one sentence or phrase to "hang on to" for the week. Here are some ideas:

   • "We pray that we will use what we are given wisely, remembering especially the poor and the needy."

   • "We pray that a new and right spirit will be put within us."

   • "We ask for the grace to treat others, especially those who harm us, with the same mercy that we have received from God."

   • "No matter how bleak the world may sometimes seem, there is nonetheless a depth of love which is deeper than our despair."

   Maybe one of these, or another phrase, is particularly meaningful to you. See if you can memorize it, or at least remember the gist of it. Let this phrase stick with you through the week. Include it in your prayers, think about it while you are in the car, and remember it in the midst of a stressful situation. Look for connections between the phrase you selected and the world around you. Perhaps a conversation, a TV show, a current event, or a situation at home or at work will remind you of it. Record your thoughts and observations about this phrase and others in the journal space provided.

3. Consider using the Questions for Personal Reflection at the end of Session 6 (page 94) to reflect on last week's material if you did not already complete this exercise in class.

Group Session

OPENING PRAYER (5 MINUTES)

Have the group leader or another class member open the session with prayer. Invite those who are willing to share the catechism phrase they focused on in their journaling.

KEY BIBLICAL REFERENCES (15 MINUTES)

Guidelines

Assign individual class members the catechism questions and accompanying scripture passages listed below. Read catechism Question 130 responsively, with one person asking the question and the rest of the class reading the answer aloud in unison. (See page 95 for catechism questions.) Have the assigned class member read aloud the corresponding scripture passages. Follow this pattern for Questions 131 and 132 as well.

a. *Study Catechism* Question 130 (Matt. 6:11; Luke 11:3; Prov. 30:8; Ps. 55:22; 72:4; 90:17; 104:27–28; Ex. 16:1–21)

b. *Study Catechism* Question 131 (Matt. 6:12; Luke 11:4; Matt. 6:14–15; 18:33; Ps. 51:10; 1 John 2:1–2)

c. *Study Catechism* Question 132 (Matt. 6:13; Matt. 26:41; 2 Cor. 4:8; Eph. 3:19)

HISTORICAL AND THEOLOGICAL BACKGROUND (5–10 MINUTES)

You have three options for this section:

1. The teacher may summarize the main points of the material (found on pages 96–100) that was read by class members in preparation for the group session.

2. The teacher may ask for volunteers to share one or two important points they remember from the Historical and Theological Background section.

3. If your group is coming to this session without advance preparation, you may ask several group members to take turns reading aloud the Historical and Theological Background material (found on pages 96–100).

REFLECTIONS FOR CHRISTIANS TODAY (5 MINUTES)

Guidelines

Have several class members take turns reading aloud this section.

At each worship service we say the words of the Lord's Prayer together. They roll off our tongues effortlessly. They are as comfortable and familiar as a favorite sweater in the fall or the taste of grandmother's pound cake. How often, do you suppose, have you prayed the prayer in your lifetime? Is it possible that the old cautionary phrase "familiarity breeds contempt" is operative here? Have we become so comfortable and accustomed to the weekly ritual of reciting the Lord's Prayer in worship that it has become mere routine? Does it still have power to guide us into a deeper devotion to God as we reflect on God's graciousness?

Consider the final three petitions. Too often the prayer is said without any opportunity for reflection on the substance of the request; we hurry through, asking God to "give us," "forgive us," and "deliver us" without pausing long enough to allow God to deal with issues in our present, past, or future. What comes to mind when you pray for daily bread? Does anything, or are you already pressing on to forgiveness? Do the faces of the world's poor and needy crowd in, gaunt and staring? Are you confronted by your own needs and anxious about the stability of the economy? Or consider forgiveness. As you pray are you confronted by your own sinfulness and need for forgiveness, or do you see only those who have wronged you? Do you feel like running to God or away from God? And with the final petition, is there time to contemplate the trials we confront and the evil we face? Perhaps the weekly communal offering of the Lord's Prayer may work on us to pull apart the petitions and, in the privacy of personal prayer, to slow down and go deeper with God.

The catechism invites us to pause and ponder again God's graciousness evidenced in the second section of the Lord's Prayer. *"Along with every living creature we look to God, the source of all generosity, to bless us and nourish us, according to the divine good pleasure" (SC#130).* The promise for blessing and nourishment encompasses both our physical and spiritual needs. Jesus offers these three petitions in this model prayer as a way we can bring the needs of our life to God. If we move beyond saying them as ritual and make them real, we may experience firsthand both their power and God's pleasure.

QUESTIONS FOR SMALL-GROUP REFLECTION AND DISCUSSION
(20 MINUTES)

Guidelines

Divide into groups of three to five persons to discuss one or two of the following groups of questions. We recommend that you select only one or two questions in order to have a more in-depth discussion. If your group finishes discussing the questions before the allotted time has passed, feel free to move on to another question.

1. Select one of the last three petitions in the Lord's Prayer. Read the relevant catechism section (SC#130–132). Share why you selected that phrase and what it means to you.

2. What does it mean to you that Jesus instructs us to ask God for what we need?

3. *"God commands us to pray each day for all that we need and no more, so that we will learn to rely completely on God" (SC#130).* Reflect on the difference between our "needs" and our "wants"— consider your answer in light of the hymn that sings: "Hast thou not seen/How thy desires e'er have been/Granted in what He ordaineth?"[16]

4. The *Study Catechism* affirms that when we petition God for forgiveness we are asking *"that a new and right spirit will be put within us" (SC#131).* How does this help you to understand forgiveness? What does it mean to pray for a new and right spirit?

5. The sixth petition speaks of the temptation of *"yield[ing] to despair in the face of seemingly hopeless circumstances" (SC#132).* How does your church celebrate the mighty acts of God that help the community sustain hope?

Case Studies (20 minutes)

Guidelines

Divide the class into groups of three to five persons to read and discuss the following case studies. Assign Case Study #1 to half the groups and Case Study #2 to the other half.

1. The presbytery's Hunger Action enabler recently met with the mission committee of your church and shared information regarding the relative daily diet of Presbyterians in your presbytery and that of Presbyterians in your partner churches in Ghana, West Africa. She indicated that the people in the partner churches get by on about one-third fewer calories per day. The mission committee, responding to this information and desiring both to raise awareness in your church and to be in solidarity with the Ghanaians, petitioned the session to have all Wednesday night church suppers be subsistence meals. The money saved on the cost of preparing the meals would be sent to support the presbytery's hunger program. *How would you use the catechism commentary on the fourth petition, along with biblical references, to handle the mission committee's request?*

2. A discussion arose at the monthly circle meeting about the former pastor, who left under some duress five years ago. The congregation was polarized with regard to the pastor and the division is still visible. The vote to sever the pastoral relationship left a rift running down the center aisle. Where you sat in church (on the pulpit side or on the lectern side) made it clear to everyone else where you had stood on the issue of whether the pastor should stay or go. "I still don't know how anyone could have voted against our pastor!" one of the longtime members complained. "He was the kindest man and gave the best sermons and was always out visiting in the home. The church hasn't been the same since he left. I don't know if I can ever forgive those members who were so cruel as to kick him out." As she was speaking, another woman in the circle began to look very uncomfortable. Finally, she could not contain herself any longer and said with a voice choked with anger and emotion, "You have no idea how difficult it is for me to be here because of that man! He nearly destroyed my faith and trust in God because of an 'inappropriate relationship' he had with my neighbor. I was the only one she could tell, and I couldn't tell anyone. Sitting in church on Sunday was horrible. God seemed so distant. How could that man pray the prayers of confession and grant the congregation forgiveness when he was causing so much evil. I was the one who finally had to go to the committee on ministry. I don't know if I can ever forgive him for what he did or forgive myself for blowing the whistle on him and causing the split in the church." *Both of these women express issues regarding forgiveness. How are they alike? How are they different? How would you use the catechism Questions 131 and 132 along with biblical references to help them in accepting forgiveness and granting forgiveness? If you were on the committee on ministry, what word would you say to the new pastor?*

CLOSING PRAYER (5 MINUTES)

Close with a bidding prayer where the leader speaks each petition of the Lord's Prayer and the rest of the class adds particular requests. Start off by praying the first part of the Lord's Prayer, but take each of the first three petitions very slowly, pausing after each one. When you get to the second section of the prayer, say:

"Loving God, in the days of his earthly ministry your Son taught us to boldly bring our needs to you.

So we pray:

> Give us today . . .

> Forgive us . . .

> Deliver us . . . ."

(Allow time for class members to fill in each petition before going on to the next one.)

Conclude the prayer with the closing doxology, "For the kingdom, the power and the glory are yours now and for ever. Amen."

Optional Exercises

These optional exercises may be included as part of the group session following the case-study discussion. Alternatively, class members may use the Questions for Personal Reflection to add to their journaling during their time between classes.

QUESTIONS FOR PERSONAL REFLECTION (20 MINUTES)

Guidelines

Invite group members to reflect individually and silently on one or more of these questions. Allow at least ten minutes of quiet. Come back together as a group and invite members to share some of their thoughts. Allow ten minutes for sharing.

1. Imagine you are one of the disciples to whom Jesus first taught this prayer. Hear him instruct you to pray for your own needs in these petitions. Remember that Peter and Judas are with you receiving instruction. How does this change your view of the prayer? Does it?

2. When praying, "Give us today our daily bread," we *"ask God to provide for all our needs, for we know that God, who cares for us in every area of our life, has promised us temporal as well as spiritual blessings" (SC#130).* What do you need from God temporally and spiritually? Which need is most pressing?

3. Reflect on a time when it has been difficult to pray, "Forgive us our sins as we forgive those who sin against us." Is there someone you need to forgive to fully experience God's forgiveness in your own life?

4. Which of your *"own worst impulses and . . . external powers of destruction in the world" (SC#132)* do you need to be delivered from?

5. Have you experienced the *"depth of [God's] love which is deeper than our despair" (SC#132)?* Reflect on Colossians 1:12–23, which celebrates the triumph of God's love.

Optional Artistic Application (20 minutes)

Guidelines

Instead of the Small-Group Reflection and Discussion questions listed on pages 104–105, you may choose to have the class divide into small groups of three to five persons for this exercise. Provide sufficient magazines for your class to make collages. Include a diversity of choices, from weekly newsmagazines and cooking magazines to magazines focusing on sports and business. Invite the class to cut out pictures that would represent the three petitions found in the second part of the Lord's Prayer and paste them onto the construction paper you provide. Have them share and discuss their collages.

For Further Reading

Bondi, Roberta. Preface and Chapters 4–6 in *A Place to Pray: Reflections of the Lord's Prayer*. Nashville: Abingdon Press, 1996.

Postema, Don. "Wrestling with God" and "Prayer as Justice/Compassion." Chapters 7–8 in *Space for God: The Study and Practice of Prayer and Spirituality*. Grand Rapids, Mi.: CRC Publications, 1994.

Smedes, Lewis. Parts 1 and 4 in *Forgive and Forget*. San Francisco: Harper San Francisco, 1996.

Thompson, Marjorie J. "Communication and Communion with God." Chapter 3 in *Soul Feast: An Invitation to the Christian Spiritual Life*. Louisville, Ky.: Westminster/John Knox Press, 1995.

Willimon, William H., and Stanley Hauerwas. Introduction and Chapters 6–8 in *Lord, Teach Us: The Lord's Prayer & the Christian Life*. Nashville: Abingdon Press, 1996.

Wright, N.T. Chapters 3–4 in *The Lord & His Prayer*. Grand Rapids, Mi.: Wm. B. Eerdmans Publishing Company, 1996.

SESSION 8

Celebrating Our Faith and Confidence in God

Theme:

This session will focus on the concluding line of the Lord's Prayer and reflect on the meaning of "Amen."

The *Study Catechism:* Questions 133–134

> ***Question 133. What is meant by the closing doxology, "For the kingdom, the power and the glory are yours now and for ever"?***
>
> We give God thanks and praise for the kingdom more powerful than all enemies, for the power perfected in the weakness of love, and for the glory that includes our well-being and that of the whole creation, both now and to all eternity. We give thanks and praise to God as made known through Christ our Lord.
>
> ***Question 134. What is meant by the word "Amen"?***
>
> "Amen" means "so be it" or "let it be so." It expresses our complete confidence in the triune God, the God of the covenant with Israel as fulfilled through our Lord Jesus Christ, who makes no promise that will not be kept, and whose steadfast love and mercy endures forever.

Individual Preparation

Read the catechism questions and answers above and then read the Historical and Theological Background section. Suggestions for Keeping a Journal follow this section.

The Lord's Prayer trains our attention "upward" to God in the first three petitions and then "inward" and "outward" to our personal needs and relationships in the last three petitions. It invites us to conclude by singing a doxology. Each Sunday as the church gathers for worship, it rehearses the proper relationship between creature and Creator.[1] During the service, the congregation gathers its various voices into one voice and sings a song of praise to God that affirms the order of the relationship. The familiar notes of "Old Hundredth" are sounded as the congregation stands together to tell the truth about who we are and whose we are:

> Praise God, from whom all blessings flow;
> Praise God, all creatures here below;
> Praise God above, ye heavenly host;
> Praise Father, Son, and Holy Ghost. Amen.

Like a great centering psalm, the Doxology orients us to the object of our worship—the triune God—and reminds us that, as we saw in Session 1, the ultimate goal of human life is to "glorify" God and "enjoy" God forever.[2] In a similar way, the doxology at the end of the Lord's Prayer draws our collective attention back from the particular "trials" and "evil" from which we have prayed to be delivered, and orients us, as Calvin puts it, to the "firm and tranquil repose for our faith . . . [the assurance that the] Kingdom, power, and glory can never be taken away from our Father."[3]

Ending in Praise

One of the issues that a study of the Lord's Prayer raises is the origin of the concluding doxology. In both Matthew (6:13) and Luke (11:4), Jesus concludes the prayer with the ominous words of the sixth petition. The words, "for the kingdom, the power and the glory are yours now and for ever" are not found in the original Gospel text. For Calvin, the addition of the doxology is appropriate since it reminds those who pray the petitions to be "bold to ask and . . . confident of receiving."[4] The doxology was introduced for liturgical use in worship where the congregation would say, or sing, these words in response to the priest's saying each of the six petitions. In the second century, church leaders placed the doxology at its present position because of the natural connection with the sixth petition. Placing it right after the petition "deliver us" says, in effect, "Show yourself, O God, to be the King, powerful and glorious, by delivering us from evil."[5] Moreover, finishing the prayer with the sixth petition would mean ending with a word about us, rather than in praise of God. But with the doxology our focus is drawn like metal to a magnet to the word "yours." God is willing and able to do everything we have asked in this prayer. "It may not be authentic historically," observes Douglas John Hall about the addition of the doxology, "but it is entirely appropriate theologically and ethically."[6]

In the closing doxology *"we give God thanks and praise for the kingdom more powerful than all enemies" (SC#133).* The Gospel witnesses to this truth from the beginning. "In those days," run Luke's well-worn words, "a decree went out from Emperor Augustus that all the world should be registered" (Luke 2:1). The story has become so familiar that unless we pause to reflect we may overlook what Luke is trying to communicate. In just fourteen verses that are read every Christmas, Luke moves from the emperor in Rome to the new King who is to rule the world. For Luke and the early church, the shepherds quaked and the angels sang not for a ruler in Rome, but for the Potentate of time.[7]

Yet, Jesus came into the world not with the pomp and privilege of the power standards of this world, but with all the vulnerability of a homeless child. The poet John Donne captures this in his poem "Epiphany":

> The whole life of Christ was a continual Passion; others die martyrs but Christ was born a martyr. He found a Golgotha even in Bethlehem, where he was born; for to his tenderness then the straws were almost as sharp as the thorns after, and the manger as uneasy at first as his cross at last. His birth and his death were but one continual act, and his Christmas Day and his Good Friday are but the evening and morning of one and the same day. And as even his birth is his death, so every action and passage that manifests Christ to us is his birth, for *Epiphany is manifestation.*[8]

In Christ's coming, we see *"power perfected in the weakness of love" (SC#133).* As the Suffering Servant comes into the world, the cross looms large against the crèche, and the stark image of Calvary intrudes into Christmas. "No one has greater love than this, to lay down one's life for one's friends" (John 15:13). The apostle Paul bears witness to God's way not being the world's way. Preaching about the cross is "a stumbling block to Jews and foolishness to Gentiles, but to those who are the called, both Jews and Greeks, Christ the power of God and the wisdom of God. For God's foolishness is wiser than human wisdom, and God's weakness is stronger than human strength" (1 Cor. 1:23–25). The doxology invites us to join our voices to sing:

> Blessing and honor and glory and power,
> Wisdom and riches and strength evermore,
> Give we to Christ who our battle has won,
> Whose are the kingdom, the crown and the throne.
>
> Give we the glory and praise to the Lamb;
> Take we the robe and the harp and the palm;
> Sing we the song of the Lamb that was slain,
> Dying in weakness but rising to reign.
>
> HORATIUS BONAR, 1866[9]

We are to trust our lives completely to God in all circumstances we face, because "he who has promised is faithful" (Heb. 10:23). We know this because of the character of God who has been for us all along. God did not abandon us when we fell into sin, but "if we are faithless, he remains faithful—for he cannot deny himself" (2 Tim. 2:13). God chose the people of Israel for the sake of all humanity. And when Israel rebelled, God sent Jesus Christ to fulfill the covenant with Israel, for the sake of Israel and for us all. God can be trusted to make "all things work together for good" (Rom. 8:28), now and forever. As we seek to persevere in the Christian life, even while facing "trials" and "evil," we are sustained by affirming the trustworthiness of God.

Say "Amen," Somebody!

For the Reformers, the "Amen" teaches us not to doubt when we pray but to believe, because it *"means 'so be it' or 'let it be so'"* *(SC#134).* Calvin suggests that in saying "Amen" we "express the warmth of desire to obtain what we have asked of God."[10] This *"complete confidence in the triune God"* is the basis for saying "Amen" for Luther, since "this word is nothing else than an unquestioning affirmation of faith on the part of one who does not pray as a matter of chance but knows that God does not lie since [God] has promised to grant our requests."[11] "Amen" means we take the whole prayer seriously; it is an affirmation to all that has been prayed already.

The Heidelberg Catechism also concludes by inquiring about the meaning of the "little word 'Amen'" and teaches that it means: "this shall truly and certainly be. For my prayer is much more certainly heard by God than I am persuaded in my heart that I desire such thing from [God]."[12] So "Amen" signifies our strengthened hope. A hope based not on our worth or faith but placed solely in *"our Lord Jesus Christ, who makes no promise that will not be kept, and whose steadfast love and mercy endures forever" (SC#134).*

Finally, the "Amen" reminds us that nothing can "separate us from the love of God in Christ Jesus our Lord" (Rom. 8:39). We bear witness to this reality on Christ the King Sunday, the last day of the liturgical year, when the liturgy celebrates our Lord's reign and invites us to sing:

Come, lift your hearts on high;
    Alleluia! Amen!
Let praises fill the sky;
    Alleluia! Amen!
He is our guide and friend;
    To us He'll condescend;
His love shall never end;
    Alleluia! Amen!

Praise yet our Christ again;
    Alleluia! Amen!
Life shall not end the strain;
    Alleluia! Amen!
On heaven's blissful shore
    His goodness we'll adore,
Singing forevermore,
    "Alleluia! Amen!"

CHRISTIAN HENRY BATEMAN, 1843[13]

KEEPING A JOURNAL

1. Focus on the word "Amen" and list the affirmations that provide certainty for you. Ask God for help in areas where you are less certain, areas of struggle where your "Amen" is weak. Can you trust God even with those areas of uncertainty?

2. Reread the catechism questions and answers for this session. Choose one sentence or phrase to "hang on to" for the week. Here are some ideas:

   • "the power perfected in the weakness of love"

   • "the glory that includes our well-being and that of the whole creation, both now and to all eternity"

   • "our Lord Jesus Christ, who makes no promise that will not be kept, and whose steadfast love and mercy endures forever"

   Maybe one of these, or another phrase, is particularly meaningful to you. See if you can memorize it, or at least remember the gist of it. Let this phrase stick with you through the week. Include it in your prayers, think about it while you are in the car, and remember it in the midst of a stressful situation. Look for connections between the phrase you selected and the world around you. Perhaps a conversation, a TV show, a current event, or a situation at home or at work will remind you of it. Record your thoughts and observations about this phrase and others in the journal space provided.

3. Consider using the Questions for Personal Reflection at the end of Session 7 (pages 107–108) to reflect on last week's material if you did not already complete this exercise in class.

_____

_____

_____

_____

_____

_____

_____

_____

_____

_____

_____

_____

_____

_____

_____

_____

_____

_____

_____

_____

_____

_____

_____

_____

_____

_____

_____

_____

_____

Group Session

OPENING PRAYER (5 MINUTES)

Have the group leader or another class member open the session with prayer. Invite those who are willing to share the catechism phrase they focused on in their journaling.

KEY BIBLICAL REFERENCES (15 MINUTES)

Guidelines

Assign individual class members the catechism questions and accompanying scripture passages listed below. Read catechism Question 133 responsively, with one person asking the question and the rest of the class reading the answer aloud in unison. (See page 109 for catechism questions.) Have the assigned class member read aloud the corresponding scripture passages. Follow this pattern for Question 134 as well.

a. *Study Catechism* Question 133 (Rev. 4:11, 5:12; 1 Chron. 29:11, 13)

b. *Study Catechism* Question 134 (Rev. 22:20; 2 Cor. 1:20; 2 Tim. 2:13)

HISTORICAL AND THEOLOGICAL BACKGROUND (5–10 MINUTES)

You have three options for this section:

1. The teacher may summarize the main points of the material (found on pages 110–113) that was read by class members in preparation for the group session.

2. The teacher may ask for volunteers to share one or two important points they remember from the Historical and Theological Background section.

3. If your group is coming to this session without advance preparation, you may ask several group members to take turns reading aloud the Historical and Theological Background material (found on pages 110–113).

REFLECTIONS FOR CHRISTIANS TODAY (5 MINUTES)

Guidelines

Have several class members take turns reading aloud this section.

We live in a narcissistic culture, which has developed a cult of the self. In the vernacular of the day, so much is "about us." The individual is exalted over the community, even as the creature is honored instead of the Creator. Increasingly people are giving up on the difficult work of building healthy communities and strengthening neighborhoods and becoming ever more self-absorbed and self-sufficient. The Lord's Prayer is a guard against this movement and a guide for those who want to follow Christ rather than cultural trends. The prayer gives voice to our hope that God's reign will be established soon and take effect already in our lives. Jesus came preaching the good news that the kingdom of God was at hand. His work and words made the presence and power of God's gracious rule felt. Thus the petitions "hallowed be your name; your kingdom come, your will be done, on earth as in heaven" are prayed in gratitude for the victory of God in Jesus Christ even while we wait for the final unveiling of God's cosmic triumph. Such petitions nurture lives of humility and confidence and hope— lives lived out under the sign of the cross, out of the power of the resurrection, and toward the new age of God's peaceable kingdom. These petitions are not otherworldly or individualistic. We are not asking to be rescued from the world or from our communities. Rather, we are asking confidently, hopefully, and humbly that God will reign in our world and in our communities.

Honesty in such a prayer will have significant social effects. If, with these petitions, we yearn for the final consummation of God's victory in Christ, the final destruction of evil, the complete surrender of those principalities and powers that alienate people from God and from one another, then we must live in hope and action. We must be "straining forward to what lies ahead" (Phil. 3:13). If we pray in gratitude and hope for God's victory, then in the interim between resurrection and consummation we must fight the good fight, we must enlist in the battle against human suffering, against hunger and sickness, against war and poverty, against human injustice, against economic inequities and political tyrannies, against racial prejudice and international exploitation. We turn away from the narcissism of the culture because *"the kingdom [is] more powerful than all enemies, . . . and [we give God thanks] for the glory that includes our well-being and that of the whole creation" (SC#133).*

QUESTIONS FOR SMALL-GROUP REFLECTION AND DISCUSSION (20 MINUTES)

Guidelines

Divide into groups of three to five persons to discuss one or two of the following groups of questions. We recommend that you select only one or two questions in order to have a more in-depth discussion. If your group finishes discussing the questions before the allotted time has passed, feel free to move on to another question.

1. Select either the closing doxology or the concluding "Amen." Read the relevant catechism section (SC Questions 133–134) and share why you selected the particular phrase and what it means to you.

2. Consider how the closing doxology informs the whole of the catechism, and how it works as a punctuation mark for the document and the Christian life. What difference does this insight make to you and your church community?

3. The doxology affirms that we *"give God . . . praise for the kingdom more powerful than all enemies, for the power perfected in the weakness of love" (SC#133).* What enemies does your church community confront? Where do you see power perfected in the weakness of love?

4. *"Amen". . . expresses our complete confidence in the triune God, . . . who makes no promise that will not be kept" (SC#134).* It is sometimes said that the church's future is as bright as the promises of God. What are the bedrock promises that ground our hope as we enter the third millennium?

5. How has the *"steadfast love and mercy"* of *"the God of the covenant with Israel as fulfilled through our Lord Jesus Christ" (SC#134)* been experienced in your life and in the life of your church community?

CASE STUDIES (20 MINUTES)

Guidelines

Divide the class into groups of three to five persons to read and discuss the following case studies. Assign Case Study #1 to half the groups and Case Study #2 to the other half.

1. You have been asked to visit some of the church's homebound members. The pastor and chairperson of the congregational nurture committee gave you basic instruction in how to care for the people you will visit. The notebook they handed out even contained a number of written prayers appropriate for visiting the sick. You were especially charged to pray with those you encounter. Mr. Jones is your first stop. A lifelong member of the church, now in his late seventies, he is being treated for prostate cancer. You conclude your time together by inviting him to pray and offering one of the printed prayers from your book. The prayer leaves Mr. Jones reflective. "Thank you," he says. "I find it hard to pray. Who should I pray to? Our heavenly Father, Jesus, or the Holy Spirit?" *How would you answer Mr. Jones? Based on the catechism understanding that "Amen*

. . . expresses our complete confidence in the triune God," what would you tell him? What biblical references are helpful in giving you guidance?

2. The worship committee of session has been seeking to respond sensitively to those in the congregation who would like to add a less formal service of worship. A few other churches in your community have added alternative services of a contemporary nature, which have grown in popularity and received significant publicity. You have been asked to serve on the task force to plan and implement such a service in your church. At the first planning meeting, one of the young adults suggests omitting the singing of the Doxology. "Its just so *traditional*," she laments. "We sing it every week, and I'm just tired of it! Why can't we just sing something else?" *Can we sing something else? Is there a difference between singing the Doxology and a doxology? How does the catechism help you in understanding the role of the Doxology in the life and worship of God's people?*

CLOSING PRAYER (5 MINUTES)

As you close this last session with prayer, provide an opportunity for participants to offer thanks for one truth or insight they have learned in their class. See the Optional Exercises if you would like to close with a hymn.

Optional Exercises

These optional exercises may be included as part of the group session following the case-study discussion. Alternatively, class members may use the Questions for Personal Reflection to add to their journaling between classes.

QUESTIONS FOR PERSONAL REFLECTION (20 MINUTES)

Guidelines

Invite group members to reflect individually and silently on one or more of these questions. Allow at least ten minutes of quiet. Come back together as a group and invite members to share some of their thoughts. Allow ten minutes for sharing.

1. Reflect on *"the glory that includes our well-being and that of the whole creation, both now and to all eternity" (SC#133).* What does this affirmation mean to you? Does it provide comfort or raise more questions?

2. On a scale of 1 to 5 with 1 being the lowest and 5 being the highest, how would you rate your *"complete confidence in the triune God" (SC#134)?* How can you grow in trusting God with your future?

3. What does it mean for you that in your baptism you have been claimed as "a child of the Covenant"? What does it mean for you that *"the covenant with Israel [is] fulfilled through our Lord Jesus Christ" (SC#134)?*

4. The *Study Catechism* began with a "benediction" (SC#1–4) and now ends with "Amen" (SC#134). What difference does this pattern make? How can you live between the benediction and the Amen?

MUSICAL EXPRESSION (5 MINUTES)

Guidelines

Have enough copies of the hymn "Let All Who Pray the Prayer Christ Taught" (#349 in *The Presbyterian Hymnal*) available for each member of the class to have one. Make sure someone is on hand to play the piano or have a strong singer lead. Read through the words before singing the hymn. Alternatively, you may wish to use the hymn "Glorious Things of Thee Are Spoken," which may be more easily found in other hymnals.

For Further Reading:

Bondi, Roberta. Preface and Chapter 7 in *A Place to Pray: Reflections of the Lord's Prayer.* Nashville: Abingdon Press, 1998.

Leith, John H. "A New Heaven and a New Earth" and "The Presence and the Power of God." Chapters 6–7 in *The Reformed Imperative: What the Church Has to Say That No One Else Can Say.* Philadelphia: The Westminster Press, 1988.

Loder, Ted. "Probing" and "Prayers of Commitment and Change." Chapters 1 and 6 in *Guerrillas of Grace.* San Diego: LuraMedia, 1984.

Postema, Don. "The Goal Is Glory." Chapter 9 in *Space for God: The Study and Practice of Prayer and Spirituality.* Grand Rapids, Mi.: CRC Publications, 1994.

Willimon, William H., and Stanley Hauerwas. Chapter 9 in *Lord, Teach Us: The Lord's Prayer & the Christian Life.* Nashville: Abingdon Press, 1996.

Wright, N.T. "The Power and the Glory." Chapter 6 in *The Lord & His Prayer.* Grand Rapids, Mi.: Wm. B. Eerdmans Publishing Company, 1996.

Notes

INTRODUCTION

1. From Form of Government, in *Book of Order* (Louisville, Ky.: Office of the General Assembly, 1991), G-1.0304.

SESSION 1: DISCOVERING OUR LIFE'S PURPOSE IN GOD'S PRESENCE

1. John Leith, *An Introduction to the Reformed Tradition,* rev. ed. (Atlanta: John Knox Press, 1981), pp. 97–100.

2. Bonnie Thurston, *Spiritual Life in the Early Church: The Witness of Acts and Ephesians* (Minneapolis: Fortress Press, 1993), p. 3.

3. John Calvin, *Institutes of the Christian Religion,* ed. John T. McNeill, trans. Ford Lewis Battles (Philadelphia: Westminster Press, 1960), 3.7.1.

4. Ibid., 3.1.1; 3.2.23–24.

SESSION 2: CALLED TO BE IN RIGHT RELATIONSHIP WITH GOD

1. William J. Carl, III, "The Decalogue in Liturgy, Preaching, and Life," *Interpretation,* vol. 43, no. 3, (July 1989), pp. 271–74.

2. Ibid., p. 271.

3. Leith, *Reformed Tradition,* p. 79.

4. Calvin, *Institutes,* 2.7.12, pp. 360–79.

5. Martin Luther, "The Large Catechism of Dr. Martin Luther, First Part: The Ten Commandments," in *The Book of Concord: The Confessions of the Evangelical Lutheran Church,* trans. and ed. Theodore C. Tappert, with Jaroslav Pelikan, Robert H. Fischer, and Arthur Piepkorn (Philadelphia: Fortress Press, 1959), p. 10.

6. Ibid., p. 10.

7. Brevard S. Childs, *The Book of Exodus: A Critical Theological Commentary,* rev. ed. (Louisville, Ky.: Westminster/John Knox Press, 1995), p. 409.

8. William C. Placher, *The Domestication of Transcendence* (Louisville, Ky: Westminster John Knox Press, 1996), p. 6.

9. Presbyterian Church (U.S.A.), *The Book of Confessions* (Louisville, Ky.: Office of the General Assembly, 1991), 3.01.

10. Calvin, *Institutes,* 2.7.23, p. 389.

11. *Book of Confessions,* 4.099.

12. Karl Barth, *Church Dogmatics,* vol. 3, *The Doctrine of Creation,* pt. 4, ed. A.T. Mackay et al. (Edinburgh: T & T Clark, 1961), p. 50.

13. Don Postema, *Space for God: The Study and Practice of Prayer and Spirituality* (Grand Rapids, Mi.: CRC Publications, 1994), is a wonderful resource for helping create "space for God."

14. Paul Hanson, *The People Called: The Growth of Community in the Bible* (San Francisco: Harper & Row, 1986), p. 53. See discussion of the Decalogue as a guide for small groups in Gareth Weldon Icenogle, *Biblical Foundations for Small Group Ministry: An Integrational Approach* (Downers Grove, Ill.: InterVarsity Press, 1994), pp. 46–66.

15. From "Dear Lord and Father of Mankind," sts. 3 and 4, *The Presbyterian Hymnal* (Louisville, Ky.: Westminster/John Knox Press, 1990), hymn 345.

Session 3: Called to Be in Right Relationship with One Another

1. Luther, "Large Catechism," p. 379.

2. Calvin, *Institutes,* 1.8.35, p. 401.

3. Luther, "Large Catechism," p. 389.

4. Ibid., p. 393

5. Calvin, *Institutes,* 1.8.39, p. 404

6. Terrence E. Fretheim, *Exodus, Interpretation: A Bible Commentary for Teaching and Preaching* (Louisville, Ky.: John Knox Press, 1993), p. 221.

Session 4: Living as a People of Faith in the World

1. Luther, "Large Catechism," p. 395.

2. Ibid., p. 399.

3. Calvin, *Institutes,* 1.8.47, p. 411.

4. John I. Durham, *Exodus,* vol. 3 in *Word Biblical Commentary* (Waco, Tex.: Word Books, 1987), p. 298.

5. Calvin, *Institutes,* 1.8.49, p. 413.

6. Fretheim, *Exodus,* p. 235.

7. Calvin, *Institutes,* 1.8.47, p. 411.

8. Ibid.

9. Fretheim, *Exodus,* p. 238.

10. Luther, "Large Catechism," p. 407.

Session 5: The Gift of Prayer

1. Barth, *Church Dogmatics,* vol. 3, *The Doctrine of Creation,* pt. 4, p. 98.

2. Elsee Ann McKee, "John Calvin's Teachings on the Lord's Prayer," in *The Lord's Prayer: Perspective of Reclaiming Christian Prayer,* ed. Daniel Migliore (Grand Rapids, Mi.: Wm. B. Eerdmans Publishing Company, 1993), p. 93.

3. Daniel L. Migliore, "Preface," in *The Lord's Prayer*, p. 1.

4. Ibid.

5. McKee, "John Calvin's Teachings," p. 95.

6. Migliore, "Preface," p. 2.

7. Jan Milic Lochman, "The Lord's Prayer: Perspective for Reclaiming Christian Prayer," in Migliore, *The Lord's Prayer*, p. 18.

SESSION 6: SEEKING TO BE IN COMMUNION WITH GOD

1. McKee, "John Calvin's Teaching," p. 95.

2. Ibid., p. 97.

3. Karlfried Froelich, "The Lord's Prayer in Patristic Literature," in Migliore, *The Lord's Prayer*, p. 82.

4. Barth, *Church Dogmatics*, vol. 3, *The Doctrine of Creation*, pt. 4, p. 87.

SESSION 7: DEEPENING OUR DEVOTION TO GOD

1. Frederick Dale Brunner, *The Christbook*: *A Historical/Theological Commentary, Matthew 1–12* (Waco, Tx.: Word Books, 1987), p. 249.

2. Luther, "Large Catechism," p. 72.

3. Calvin, *Institutes,* 3.20.44

4. Luther, "Large Catechism," p. 74. To emphasize the connection between the fourth petition and the role of government to ensure peace, Luther suggested that: "It would therefore be fitting if the coat-of-arms of every upright prince were emblazoned with a loaf of bread instead of a lion or a wreath of rue, or if a loaf of bread were stamped on coins, to remind both princes and subjects that through the office of the princes we enjoy protection and peace and that without them we could not have the steady blessing of daily bread" (p. 75).

5. Calvin, *Institutes,* 3.20.44.

6. Ibid., 3.20.45.

7. Ibid.

8. Luther, "Large Catechism," p. 89.

9. *Book of Confessions,* 9.31.

10. From "A Mighty Fortress Is Our God," by Martin Luther, *The Presbyterian Hymnal,* hymn 259.

11. Karl Barth, *Prayer and Preaching*. Trans. B. E. Hooks (Guildford and London: SCM Press Ltd., 1964), pp. 58–60.

12. From "I Greet Thee, Who My Sure Redeemer Art," attrib. to John Calvin, *The Presbyterian Hymnal,* hymn 457.

13. *Book of Confessions,* 4.001.

14. Barth, *Prayer and Preaching,* p. 60.

15. *Book of Confessions,* 9.54.

16. From "Praise Ye the Lord, the Almighty," by Joachim Neander, *The Presbyterian Hymnal*, hymn 482.

SESSION 8: CELEBRATING OUR FAITH AND CONFIDENCE IN GOD

1. In his monumental work *Doxology: The Praise of God in Worship, Doctrine, and Life* (New York: Oxford University Press, 1980), Geoffrey Wainwright argues that "the proper relationship between creature and Creator is, in Christian eyes, the relationship of worship" (p. 16). For Wainwright, worship is "the point of concentration at which the whole of the Christian life comes to ritual focus" (p. 8). The whole of Christian life is premised on humanity's being made in the image of God and takes expression in three "strands . . . : the human vocation to communion with God; the human task upon God's earth; the constitution of humanity as a social creature" (p. 16).

2. Walter Brueggemann offers a particularly helpful typology of the psalms in *The Message of the Psalms: A Theological Commentary* (Minneapolis: Augsburg Fortress, 1984) when he suggests there are psalms of "orientation," "disorientation," and "reorientation" (chaps. 1–3). The "psalms of orientation" work to center us as creature before our Creator.

3. Calvin, *Institutes*, 3.20.47.

4. Ibid.

5. Barth, *Prayer and Preaching*, p. 62.

6. Douglas John Hall, "The Theology and Ethics of the Lord's Prayer," in Migliore, *The Lord's Prayer*, p. 135. Hall expands on the implication of the appropriateness of the inclusion of doxology:

> "Thine is the kingdom, the power, and the glory, for ever and ever." This is the "glimpse," the world and all life, seen through the small window of faith, which enables the disciple community to be honest about what is wrong. This is the "already" that permits the church to be utterly realistic about the "not yet" (p. 135).

7. N.T. Wright, *The Lord & His Prayer* (Grand Rapids, Mi.: Wm. B. Eerdmans Publishing Company; Cincinnati, Oh.: Forward Movement Publications, 1996), provides an insightful Advent sermon on the closing doxology of the Lord's Prayer in "The Power and the Glory," pp. 77–89. He suggests that if we are serious about making Jesus' agenda our own, there are three ways to pray the final clause: a prayer of "mission and commission," a prayer of "incarnation and empowerment," and, finally, a prayer of "confidence and commitment" (pp. 86–88).

8. John Donne, "Epiphany," in *The Book of Uncommon Prayer*, ed. Constance Pollock and Daniel Pollock (Dallas, Tex.: Word Publishing, 1996), p. 49.

9. *The Presbyterian Hymnal*, hymn 147.

10. Calvin, *Institutes*, 3.20.47.

11. Luther, "Large Catechism," p. 120.

12. *Book of Confessions*, 4.129.

13. From "Come, Christians, Join to Sing," *The Presbyterian Hymnal*, hymn 150.